PHILLIS
WHEATLEY

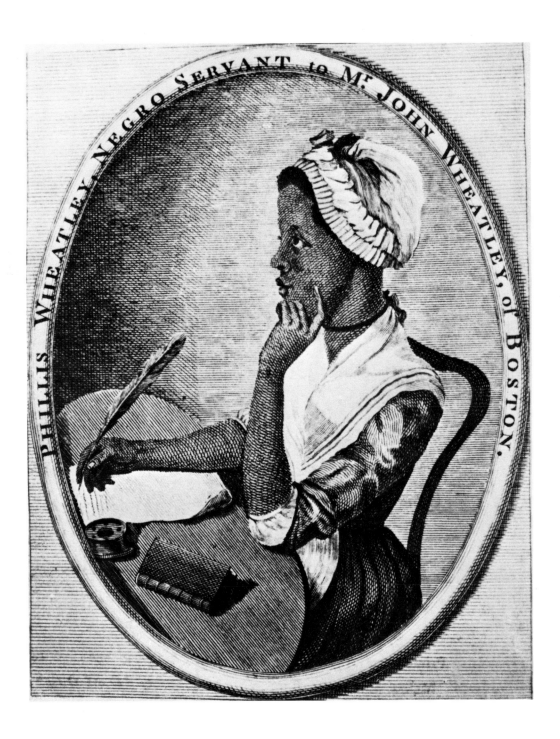

PHILLIS WHEATLEY, NEGRO SERVANT to Mr. JOHN WHEATLEY, of BOSTON.

PHILLIS WHEATLEY

MERLE RICHMOND

CHELSEA HOUSE PUBLISHERS

NEW YORK • PHILADELPHIA

EDITOR-IN-CHIEF: Nancy Toff
EXECUTIVE EDITOR: Remmel T. Nunn
MANAGING EDITOR: Karyn Gullen Browne
COPY CHIEF: Juliann Barbato
PICTURE EDITOR: Adrian G. Allen
ART DIRECTOR: Giannella Garrett
MANUFACTURING MANAGER: Gerald Levine

Staff for PHILLIS WHEATLEY:

SENIOR EDITOR: Elisa Petrini
TEXT EDITOR: Marian W. Taylor
ASSISTANT EDITOR: Maria Behan
EDITORIAL ASSISTANT: Karen Schimmel
COPYEDITORS: Terrance Dolan, Ellen Scordato
PICTURE RESEARCHER: Elie Perter
DESIGNER: Design Oasis
PRODUCTION COORDINATOR: Laura McCormick
COVER ILLUSTRATION: Jane Sterrett

CREATIVE DIRECTOR: Harold Steinberg

15 14 13 12

Library of Congress Cataloging in Publication Data

Richmond, M. A. (Merle A.) PHILLIS WHEATLEY

(American women of achievement)
Bibliography: p.
Includes index.
1. Wheatley, Phillis, 1753–1784—Biography—Juvenile literature.
2. Poets, American—18th century—Biography—Juvenile literature.
[1. Wheatley, Phillis, 1753–1784. 2. Poets, American. 3. Afro-
Americans—Biography] I. Title. II. Series.
PS866.W5Z683   1987   811'.1 [B] [92]   87-6626

ISBN 1-55546-683-4
     0-7910-0218-7 (pbk.)

CONTENTS

AMERICAN WOMEN of ACHIEVEMENT

Abigail Adams
women's rights advocate

Jane Addams
social worker

Louisa May Alcott
author

Marian Anderson
singer

Susan B. Anthony
woman suffragist

Ethel Barrymore
actress

Clara Barton
*founder of the American
Red Cross*

Elizabeth Blackwell
physician

Nellie Bly
journalist

Margaret Bourke-White
photographer

Pearl Buck
author

Rachel Carson
biologist and author

Mary Cassatt
artist

Agnes De Mille
choreographer

Emily Dickinson
poet

Isadora Duncan
dancer

Amelia Earhart
aviator

Mary Baker Eddy
*founder of the Christian
Science church*

Betty Friedan
feminist

Althea Gibson
tennis champion

Emma Goldman
political activist

Helen Hayes
actress

Lillian Hellman
playwright

Katharine Hepburn
actress

Karen Horney
psychoanalyst

Anne Hutchinson
religious leader

Mahalia Jackson
gospel singer

Helen Keller
humanitarian

Jeane Kirkpatrick
diplomat

Emma Lazarus
poet

Clare Boothe Luce
author and diplomat

Barbara McClintock
biologist

Margaret Mead
anthropologist

Edna St. Vincent Millay
poet

Julia Morgan
architect

Grandma Moses
painter

Louise Nevelson
sculptor

Sandra Day O'Connor
Supreme Court justice

Georgia O'Keeffe
painter

Eleanor Roosevelt
diplomat and humanitarian

Wilma Rudolph
champion athlete

Florence Sabin
medical researcher

Beverly Sills
opera singer

Gertrude Stein
author

Gloria Steinem
feminist

Harriet Beecher Stowe
author and abolitionist

Mae West
entertainer

Edith Wharton
author

Phillis Wheatley
poet

Babe Didrikson Zaharias
champion athlete

CHELSEA HOUSE PUBLISHERS

"Remember the Ladies"

MATINA S. HORNER

Remember the Ladies." That is what Abigail Adams wrote to her husband John, then a delegate to the Continental Congress, as the Founding Fathers met in Philadelphia to form a new nation in March of 1776. "Be more generous and favorable to them than your ancestors. Do not put such unlimited power in the hands of the Husbands. If particular care and attention is not paid to the Ladies," Abigail Adams warned, "we are determined to foment a Rebellion, and will not hold ourselves bound by any Laws in which we have no voice, or Representation."

The words of Abigail Adams, one of the earliest American advocates of women's rights, were prophetic. Because when we have not "remembered the ladies," they have, by their words and deeds, reminded us so forcefully of the omission that we cannot fail to remember them. For the history of American women is as interesting and varied as the history of our nation as a whole. American women have played an integral part in founding, settling, and building our country. Some we remember as remarkable women who—against great odds—achieved distinction in the public arena: Anne Hutchinson, who in the 17th century became a charismatic religious leader; Phillis Wheatley, an 18th-century black slave who became a poet; Susan B. Anthony, whose name is synonymous with the 19th-century women's rights movement, and who led the struggle to enfranchise women; and, in our own century, Amelia Earhart, the first woman to cross the Atlantic Ocean by air.

PHILLIS WHEATLEY

These extraordinary women certainly merit our admiration, but other women, "common women," many of them all but forgotten, should also be recognized for their contributions to American thought and culture. Women have been community builders; they have founded schools and formed voluntary associations to help those in need; they have assumed the major responsibility for rearing children, passing on from one generation to the next the values that keep a culture alive. These and innumerable other contributions, once ignored, are now being recognized by scholars, students, and the public. It is exciting and gratifying to realize that a part of our history that was hardly acknowledged a few generations ago is now being studied and brought to light.

In recent decades, the field of women's history has grown from obscurity to a politically controversial splinter movement to academic respectability, in many cases mainstreamed into such traditional disciplines as history, economics, and psychology. Scholars of women, both female and male, have organized research centers at such prestigious institutions as Wellesley College, Stanford University, and the University of California. Other notable centers for women's studies are the Center for the American Woman and Politics at the Eagleton Institute of Politics at Rutgers University, the Henry A. Murray Research Center for the Study of Lives, at Radcliffe College, and the Women's Research and Education Institute, the research arm of the Congressional Caucus on Women's Issues. Other scholars and public figures have established archives and libraries, such as the Schlesinger Library on the History of Women in America, at Radcliffe College, and the Sophia Smith Collection, at Smith College, to collect and preserve the written and tangible legacies of women.

From the initial donation of the Women's Rights Collection in 1943, the Schlesinger Library grew to encompass vast collections documenting the manifold accomplishments of American women. Simultaneously, the women's movement in general and the academic discipline of women's studies in particular also began with a narrow definition and gradually expanded their mandate. Early causes such as woman suffrage and social reform, abolition and organized labor were joined by newer concerns such as the history of women in business and the professions and in politics and government; the study of the family; and social issues such as health policy and education.

Women, as historian Arthur M. Schlesinger, jr., once pointed out, "have constituted the most spectacular casualty of traditional history. They have made up at least half the human race, but you could never tell that by looking at the books historians write." The new breed of historians is remedying that

8

omission. They have written books about immigrant women and about working-class women who struggled for survival in cities and about black women who met the challenges of life in rural areas. They are telling the stories of women who, despite the barriers of tradition and economics, became lawyers and doctors and public figures.

The women's studies movement has also led scholars to question traditional interpretations of their respective disciplines. For example, the study of war has traditionally been an exercise in military and political analysis, an examination of strategies planned and executed by men. But scholars of women's history have pointed out that wars have also been periods of tremendous change and even opportunity for women, because the very absence of men on the home front enabled them to expand their educational, economic, and professional activities and to assume leadership in their homes.

The early scholars of women's history showed a unique brand of courage in choosing to investigate new subjects and take new approaches to old ones. Often, like their subjects, they endured criticism and even ostracism by their academic colleagues. But their efforts have unquestionably been worthwhile, because with the publication of each new study and book another piece of the historical patchwork is sewn into place, revealing an increasingly comprehensive picture of the role of women in our rich and varied history.

Such books on groups of women are essential, but books that focus on the lives of individuals are equally indispensable. Biographies can be inspirational, offering their readers the example of people with vision who have looked outside themselves for their goals and have often struggled against great obstacles to achieve them. Marian Anderson, for instance, had to overcome racial bigotry in order to perfect her art and perform as a concert singer. Isadora Duncan defied the rules of classical dance to find true artistic freedom. Jane Addams had to break down society's notions of the proper role for women in order to create new social institutions, notably the settlement house. All of these women had to come to terms both with themselves and with the world in which they lived. Only then could they move ahead as pioneers in their chosen callings.

Biography can inspire not only by adulation but also by realism. It helps us to see not only the qualities in others that we hope to emulate, but also, perhaps, the weaknesses that made them "human." By helping us identify with the subject on a more personal level they help us to feel that we, too, can achieve such goals. We read about Eleanor Roosevelt, for instance, who occupied a unique and seemingly enviable position as the wife of the president. Yet we can sympathize with her inner dilemma: an inherently shy woman, she had to force herself to live a most public life in order to use her position to benefit others. We may not be able to imagine ourselves having the immense poetic talent of Emily Dickinson, but from her story we can understand the challenges faced by a creative woman who was expected to fulfill many family responsibilities. And though few of us will ever reach the level of athletic accomplishment displayed by Wilma Rudolph or Babe Zaharias, we can still appreciate their spirit, their overwhelming will to excel.

A biography is a multifaceted lens. It is first of all a magnification, the intimate examination of one particular life. But at the same time, it is a wide-angle lens, informing us about the world in which the subject lived. We come away from reading about one life knowing more about the social, political, and economic fabric of the time. It is for this reason, perhaps, that the great New England essayist Ralph Waldo Emerson wrote, in 1841, "There is properly no history: only biography." And it is also why biography, and particularly women's biography, will continue to fascinate writers and readers alike.

PHILLIS WHEATLEY

George Washington surveys the field after the Battle of Trenton (New Jersey) in 1776. Deeply impressed by the stalwart general, Phillis Wheatley had written a poem about him earlier that year.

ONE

A Poet Meets a General

On a brisk March day in 1776, a steady stream of visitors filed through the headquarters of General George Washington in Cambridge, Massachusetts. The American Revolution had been in progress for almost a year, but Washington's army was still tattered, undisciplined, and lacking essential supplies.

Washington's callers included politicians and financiers—men who could provide his bedraggled forces with personnel, food, and weapons. Each waited for his brief moment with the general, whose busy schedule prevented him from spending much time with any one of them.

One visitor, slender and plainly dressed, stood apart from all the others. This caller's presence, probably little noticed by the men discussing war and politics, was remarkable for several reasons. First, she was a woman, and women in 18th-century America rarely concerned themselves with public affairs. Second, she was black, and because most blacks in colonial times were slaves or servants, they were unlikely to be found conferring with important generals. Third, she was a poet, and the voices of poets are rarely heard at any army's headquarters in any century.

Nevertheless, historical sources indicate that the recently chosen commander in chief of the Continental forces, George Washington, spent 30 minutes talking with Phillis Wheatley—a woman, a black, and a poet.

Phillis Wheatley was 23 years old. After 15 years as a slave in the house of John and Susannah Wheatley of Boston, she had been a free woman for only 2 years. Reserved, proper, and very religious, she was already well known all over New England as a gifted poet, perhaps the best in all the colonies. She had been presented in many of the

13

George Washington inspects the work of slaves at Mount Vernon, his Virginia plantation. Although he was unaccustomed to treating blacks as equals, he received Wheatley with respectful courtesy.

finest homes in Boston, where she read her poems to the leaders of white society.

That this former slave could write at all surprised most Bostonians; that her writing faithfully reflected their own white society astonished them. When she called on Washington, Wheatley was not only a local celebrity; her reputation had spread to England with the recent publication there of a volume of her poems. She was at the peak of her fame.

In civilian life, George Washington was a prosperous Virginia planter, the owner of more than 200 black slaves. Yet on this March day in 1776, four months before the Declaration of Independence was signed, he had invited Wheatley to come to his headquarters and treated her with the same respect he might have shown an "equal."

The seeds of this unusual meeting had been planted months earlier. On October 26, 1775, the poet had sent the

14

Colonel Joseph Reed, Washington's military secretary in 1776, later became adjutant general (chief administrative officer) of the Continental army and a member of the Continental Congress.

general a poem she had written about him. She signed the accompanying letter "Phillis Wheatley." For four months, she had heard nothing from Washington. Immersed in his preparations for upcoming battles, he apparently mislaid her letter.

On February 10, 1776, however, he mentioned it in a note to his secretary, Colonel Joseph Reed. Looking through a batch of papers he was about to throw away, he told Reed, he had rediscovered the poem. He said he had

found it impressive and had even considered having it published.

Literature was not among Washington's main interests. When he told Reed he thought Wheatley had "poetical genius," he might have been referring only to the verses she had just sent him, and not to the many other poems that had built her reputation.

He probably did not realize that the elegantly written and highly complimentary poem had been composed by a former slave. In his note to Reed, he wondered whether the poet was "Mrs. or Miss Phillis Wheatley." It was not a question that a white man would have raised about a black woman in 1776, even if she was famous. Most whites, slaveholders in particular, addressed blacks only by their first names.

When he finally replied to Wheatley on February 28, 1776, Washington apologized for his delay in responding, thanked her for the poem, and explained that he would have had it published had he not been reluctant to appear vain. "If you should ever come to Cambridge, or near headquarters," he added, "I shall be happy to see a person so favored by the Muses, and to whom nature has been so beneficent in her dispensations."

By then he seemed to have learned that she was black. He addressed her as "Miss Phillis," dropping her last name but still giving her the title of "Miss." He also referred to her poem

Washington leads his partner in a minuet, a popular dance among wealthy 18th-century Southerners. Women in Washington's society were valued more for their charm than for their intelligence.

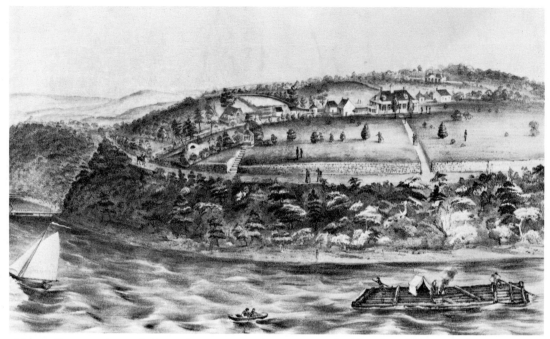

Mount Vernon, situated above the Potomac River, was worked by slave labor. Washington eventually came to view slavery as evil and directed that all his slaves be freed after his death.

as "this new instance of your genius," which suggests that he was now aware of her other writings. His letter to her probably marked the first occasion on which he had added "Miss" to a black woman's name, as well as the first time he had invited a black woman to pay him a social visit.

This kind of special treatment was not unusual for Wheatley. She had often mingled with leaders of white Boston society, although only under certain conditions and only from a certain distance. Treated differently from other blacks, she still remained apart from her white patrons. She was sus-pended between two worlds, belonging to neither.

In any case, she took far less time to accept the general's invitation than he had taken to make it. A few weeks after receiving his letter, she presented herself at his Massachusetts headquarters.

No record remains of the conversation between the general and the poet, but she apparently made a favorable impression on him. Despite his earlier misgivings, the following month her poem about him appeared in *Pennsylvania Magazine*. It was probably published on the orders of editor and patriot Thomas Paine. (Three months earlier, Paine had published *Common Sense*, a pamphlet urging immediate American independence from England. Three months later, largely because of Paine's words, the American Declaration of Independence was signed, and the shape of history was changed forever.)

Wheatley's poem about Washington contains 42 lines. It ends with a ringing tribute to the newly appointed commander:

> Proceed, great chief, with virtue on thy side,
> Thy ev'ry action let the Goddess guide.
> A crown, a mansion, and a throne that shine,
> With gold unfading, WASHINGTON! be thine.

Although, of course, neither Washington nor Wheatley could know it, when they met on that March day in 1776, both their lives were about to undergo radical change. For the military commander, there would be victory, world renown, and the adulation of his countrymen. No such glory, however, awaited the young black poet.

Thomas Paine published Wheatley's ode to Washington in his Pennsylvania Magazine *in 1776. Paine's fiery pamphlet,* Common Sense, *hastened the start of the American Revolution.*

She would face a sharp decline in her modest fortunes, ending her days ill, alone, and almost forgotten. But for one brief moment the paths of two historic figures had crossed; it was a moment whose memory Phillis Wheatley would treasure for the rest of her life.

An auctioneer takes bids on a black man in Richmond, Virginia. Although most of 18th-century America's enslaved Africans worked in the South, thousands of New Englanders also owned slaves.

TWO

Slave Child in a Strange Land

It was a summer day in 1761, and the Beach Street wharf in Boston harbor was teeming with activity, as usual. Tied to the end of the dock was the schooner *Phillis*, which had arrived after a long and hard voyage from West Africa three weeks earlier. The ship's cargo had been washed and polished and was now ready for inspection by potential buyers. The *Phillis* was a slave ship; her cargo consisted of some 75 black human beings.

Awaiting the arrival of customers was John Avery, the 50-year-old agent who had been chosen to handle the sale of the *Phillis*'s cargo. Because the quality of the shipment was poor by Yankee slave-trade standards, he was probably a bit uneasy about the success of the sale. The ship had brought too few young, able-bodied black men and too many women and children.

Timothy Fitch, the slave merchant who owned the ship, had, in fact, be-rated his captain for returning to Boston with such a "mean" cargo. Nevertheless, Avery had been enthusiastically advertising the sale in the local newspapers. Included in the "Parcel of likely Negroes" available, said the sales notices, were several "small Negroes." There was no way Avery could know that one of them would become the most famous black person in all New England.

Huddled among the slaves displayed for sale, wrote Wheatley's first biographer, Margaretta Odell, was a female child "of a slender frame, and evidently suffering from a change of climate." The little girl was naked except for a scrap of dirty carpet she had pulled around her thin body. She was, according to G. Herbert Renfro, another early chronicler, "adjudged to be seven or eight years, from the circumstance of shedding her front teeth."

Girls of that age were hard to sell

because they were not yet able to perform demanding physical tasks or to breed future slaves. Nevertheless, some slave owners considered young females a good investment because they could be easily trained to become quiet, obedient domestic servants and quickly instructed in the basic customs and practices of their masters' "Christian civilization."

On this summer morning, Susannah Wheatley, the wife of a prosperous Boston merchant, arrived at the wharf in her horse-drawn carriage. She was driven by Prince, one of the Wheatley family's slaves. The black domestics in Susannah Wheatley's household were getting old, and she was past 50 herself. Her 18-year-old twins, Mary and Nathaniel, would soon be marrying and leaving home; it was time, she had decided, to obtain a personal servant and companion to take care of her in her old age.

She was in the market for a healthy young servant, not for a sickly little girl. Nevertheless, something drew the middle-aged white woman to the black child wrapped in the carpet. Susannah Wheatley, reported biographer Odell, was touched by "the humble and modest demeanor and the interesting features of the little stranger."

John Avery must have been delighted to find a customer for this unpromising selection from his wares. After all, the child might die, adding

nothing to his receipts. In any case, he quickly made the sale, and Susannah Wheatley "procured for a trifle" the girl who would grow up to become the mother of black literature in the United States.

Peter Gwinn, captain of the *Phillis*, had arrived on the west coast of Africa several months earlier. Following the standard practice of slavers, he had toured the "factories" and "barracoons"—markets where traders, both black and white, sold their human merchandise.

Most slaves were supplied by native chiefs who acquired their captives by raiding neighboring villages. These black slavers would often set fire to a village at night, capturing its inhabitants when they fled from the flames. The chieftains would then lead their captives, tied together in long strings called "coffles," to the markets on the coast. Slavery had long been practiced in Africa, but the New World's demands for labor had vastly accelerated the hunting of human beings.

By 1800, more than 5 million slaves had been shipped from Africa to America. Although many of them died on the way (some historians put the death toll as high as 50 percent), more blacks than whites had landed in the New World by the end of the 18th century.

Phillis Wheatley, ironically named for the ship that brought her to slavery and for the family that bought her, was

Africans are unloaded from the slave ship that has brought them to the New World. Phillis Wheatley, who crossed the Atlantic on a similar vessel, was only seven years old when she arrived in Boston.

Assigned to sell the "black ivory" from the schooner Phillis, *John Avery was surprised to find a buyer for one member of his human cargo — a small black girl wrapped in a scrap of carpet.*

ently submerged beneath the trauma of her kidnapping, but she did hold on to a single recollection of that forgotten time in her native land.

In her 1834 *Memoir and Poems of Phillis Wheatley*, Margaretta Odell—who was a descendant of the Wheatley family and who had spoken to relatives who knew the poet—wrote that young Phillis kept the vision "of her mother, prostrating herself before the first golden beam that glanced across her native plains." This vivid memory suggests the Muslim ritual of welcoming the new day. But whether or not Phillis had been a Muslim in her homeland, the people of New England would soon reshape her into a devout Christian.

Phillis's survival of the ordeal of capture and transportation to America was remarkable. If she was taken aboard in Senegal, she may have spent as long as eight months on the slave ship as it sailed along the African coast and then across the Atlantic Ocean to America. Conditions aboard ships like Gwinn's were unspeakable.

The event most feared by Gwinn and other slave-ship captains was a violent uprising by their human cargoes. To prevent such revolts, they treated the captives as if they were dangerous animals. Male slaves were usually kept in chains during the 10-week Atlantic crossing, and it was made clear to all that any sign of disobedience would be dealt with mercilessly.

born on the west coast of Africa. Her exact birthplace is unknown, but the area where Gwinn picked up his cargo of slaves was Senegambia, a territory that today is divided between the nations of Senegal and Gambia.

Wheatley, who probably knew little about her ancestral roots, wrote almost nothing about her background. Some historians believe she was a member of the Fulani, a West African tribe that practiced the Muslim religion. Her personal memories of Africa were appar-

John Avery's advertisements offered to trade "small Negros" for "Negro men" who were "not of the best moral character." Slaves who proved uncooperative were often shipped to the deep South.

The slavers spoke a language that meant nothing to the imprisoned Africans, who often had no idea what orders their pale captors were giving them. They soon learned, however, that they were under the constant threat of deprivation of food, whippings, and even death.

Frail young Phillis probably lived through the grim voyage to America only because she was in a "loose pack," a cargo of no more than 80 slaves. If she had been part of a "tight pack," in which as many as 150 slaves were jammed into dark and filthy quarters in the ship's hold, she might not have survived.

During the voyage the slaves were fed a diet of rice and water. Because the traders knew that slaves—whom they called "black ivory"—brought higher prices when they were in good physical condition, they brought them up on deck for exercise twice a day. The slaves spent the rest of their time packed into the reeking hold, which lacked both sanitary facilities and room to stand upright. There was no fresh air in the sealed space below decks, and the danger of death from disease was high.

Slaves who died during the crossing were thrown overboard. Some chose to defy their white captors by starving

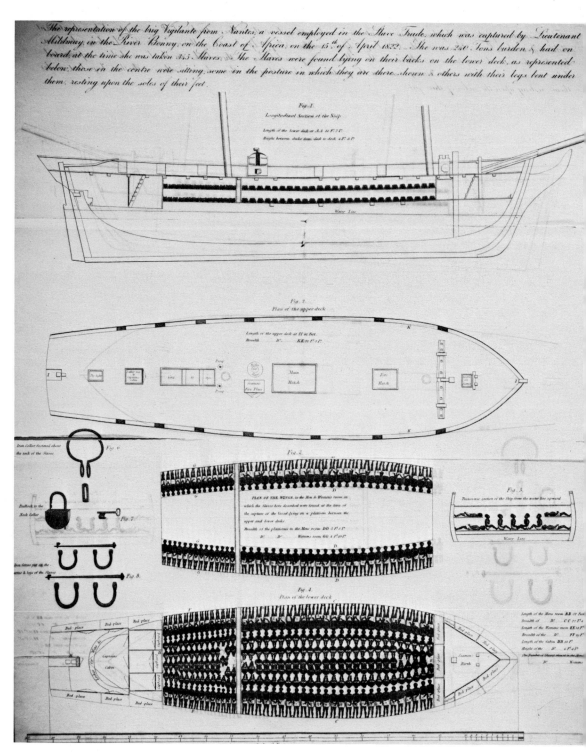

An artist who diagramed the French slave ship Vigilante reported finding some slaves "lying on their backs" and others "with their legs bent under them, resting upon the soles of their feet."

A London newspaper engraving shows young Africans aboard a slave ship. They could sleep, reported the paper, only "in a thick mass, the heads of one row resting on the hips of the next."

themselves to death or, if given the chance, by jumping overboard. One 18th-century slave-ship captain wrote in his log, "The Negroes are so wilful and loth to leave their own country that they have often leap'd . . . into the sea, and [remained] under water until they were drowned, to avoid being taken up and saved by our boats."

As far as we know, Phillis Wheatley never wrote about the specifics of slavery, but the experience of being treated so inhumanely had to have left its mark on her. She must have been confused and terrified as the slave ship plowed through the thousands of miles of

ocean that would separate her from her homeland.

The white woman who led Phillis down the wharf to the waiting carriage introduced her to a new world. Harsh words and rough treatment were now replaced with a soft voice and gentle hands. Nevertheless, the little girl was the property of another person. As a black slave, she would be ruled by her white masters. Under these circumstances, her life would be easier in the North, whose citizens at least regarded blacks as fellow human beings, than in the South, where slaves were often treated like farm animals—or worse.

At the time of Phillis Wheatley's arrival in Boston, there were about 230,000 blacks—most of them slaves—in the colonies. Only about 16,000 of these captive Africans and their descendants lived in New England; the rest worked on the South's rice, cotton, and tobacco plantations. The southern states had special laws called slave codes, which forbade blacks to own property, to defend themselves against abuse by their masters, or to testify in court against a white. Among their other provisions, the codes made it a crime to teach a black person how to read or write. It was not a crime, however, for an owner to kill a slave while punishing him.

Although a few northern slaves served as farmhands, the economy of the region was based on shipping and

Slavers prepare to sell a consignment of captured villagers at a barracoon, or slave market, on the west coast of Africa. Both blacks and whites participated in the African slave trade.

manufacturing, not on agriculture. Most of the northern blacks were employed as household servants and were usually treated less severely than their southern counterparts. New Englanders, less insistent than Southerners on the "inferiority" of blacks to themselves, allowed blacks to attend their churches. They required them, however, to worship in the "African corner," a separate section in the back of the church.

Seating the little girl she had just purchased in her carriage, Susannah Wheatley instructed Prince to drive home. The ride through the city's streets introduced the child to a strange land and a way of life radically different from anything she had ever experienced.

The pace of the city was rapid and chaotic, full of competing sights, sounds, and smells. Existence here had nothing in common with life in an African village. As Prince deftly guided the carriage through the busy daytime

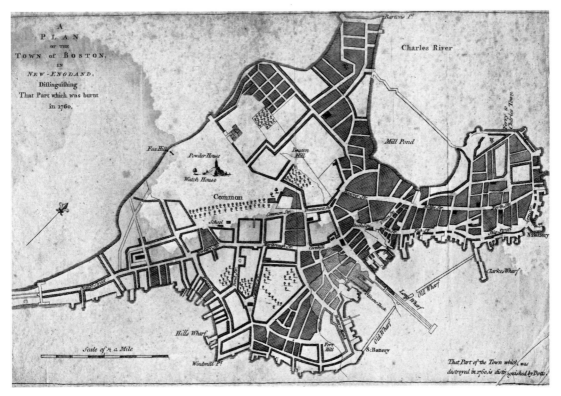

This map of Boston was made about 1761, the year of Phillis Wheatley's arrival. The city had fewer than 15,000 residents at the time, but it seemed gigantic to the little African girl.

traffic, the African child must have felt bewildered and afraid.

The streets were crowded with people of many different colors and appearances. Most of them were white, but some were black and others brown. There were seamen smartly outfitted in British, French, or Spanish uniforms. They strolled near the docks, mingling with roughly dressed sailors and deckhands. The economy of Boston was based on the sea, and the city's air was filled with the aroma of fresh fish car-

ried by the breeze blowing from the harbor.

Phillis Wheatley saw men in waistcoats, knee breeches, and white-powdered wigs, striding along with an important air. Strolling past shop windows were women wearing long, full skirts; some were trailed by servants laden with packages. Roving vendors proclaimed the virtues of their wares with loud calls and the ringing of hand bells. Others hawked their goods and services from waist-high wooden stalls.

King Street, site of the Wheatleys' home and center of Boston's cultural life, was also the scene of several violent incidents that heralded the American Revolution.

The air was filled with an array of mysterious smells: turpentine, spices, oranges, bananas, and tea and coffee shipped to the colonies from England. Through the open doors and windows of taverns came the odors of rum, cooked food, pipe tobacco, and beer.

The city's buildings, from one to three stories high, were made of brick and wood. Some were homes, some the shops of tailors, bakers, butchers, grocers, candle makers, and other merchants. Punctuating the skyline were the steeples of Boston's churches, the towers of a Christian religion that would become a major force in Phillis Wheatley's life.

Although Boston was a sprawling metropolis by the standards of the day, the city was only two miles long, an encampment on a small peninsula projecting into the harbor. It was no more than 700 yards wide at its broadest point. In 1765, four years after Phillis was taken into the Wheatley household, Boston's population was recorded at 15,520. On that first day, however, the city must have seemed to Phillis enormous and unruly, with crowds of fair-skinned people speaking in a babel of foreign tongues. Boston and Africa might have been on separate planets.

King Street (now State Street), where the stylish Wheatley mansion stood, was one of the busiest thoroughfares in Boston, the heart of the city's political, social, and commercial life. In the years to come, some of the worst of the riots that preceded the Revolution would erupt on or near King Street, but these historic events were still far from the lives of the new slave and her mistress. Prince brought the carriage to a halt in front of the big house, which would be Phillis Wheatley's home for the next 14 years.

Susannah Wheatley, a 52-year-old Christian woman of substantial means, would soon discover that she had gotten much more than she bargained for. She had wanted a personal servant; she had acquired a poet. She would spend the rest of her life promoting and supporting the talent of the black child who now stood mutely beside her.

John Hancock sat for this portrait by American painter John Singleton Copley in 1771. An early admirer of Wheatley's work, Hancock was the first signer of the Declaration of Independence.

THREE

Poetry Among Puritans

Any ordinary child, wrenched away from his or her home and plunged into a new and alien society, would feel intimidated. Phillis Wheatley was seven years old when she arrived in Boston, and the city and its white, Christian culture terrified her at first. She soon proved, however, that she was no ordinary child.

With amazing speed, she learned to understand spoken English and quickly showed an ability to grasp its written form. "She gave indications of an uncommon intelligence," wrote biographer Margaretta Odell, "and was frequently seen endeavoring to make letters upon the wall with a piece of chalk or charcoal."

Some colonists might have seen Phillis's desire to master their language as a challenge to the natural order of things. Verbal abilities such as those she was exhibiting were not, after all, expected of a child, particularly a fe-

male child. That they were being demonstrated by a child who was not only female but also black was surely extraordinary.

In most southern households, such behavior would have been severely punished. Even in many New England homes, it might have created uneasiness, but the Wheatleys were different. They found the qualities demonstrated by their young slave remarkable. John and Susannah Wheatley responded to Phillis's passion for learning with support and encouragement, not threats and punishment. They apparently saw the girl's intelligence as a blessing and believed it their duty to nurture her budding talent—especially since it belonged, in a sense, to them.

The Wheatleys assigned their 18-year-old daughter, Mary—who, like Phillis, was often in poor health herself—to serve as Phillis's childhood tutor. In contrast to the normal routine of New England slaves, Phillis's days included long periods of reading the Bible and studying poetry with Mary. Not satisfied with conquering English, Phillis would begin the study of Latin a few years later.

By the time she was 9, after only 16 months on American soil, Phillis could not only read English but could understand some of the most difficult passages in the Bible. She had already surpassed many white colonial women in learning.

The socially prominent Wheatleys treated Phillis with a respect that virtually no other slave enjoyed. Her special position, however, had drawbacks as well as advantages. While it freed her to develop and refine her artistic talent, it also separated her from the community of her own people. As one contemporary observer noted, she was not "allowed to associate with the other domestics of the family, who were of her own color and condition, but was kept constantly about the person of her mistress."

Phillis was about 12 when she began to write poems. The Wheatleys were impressed, as they were by all her displays of unusual brightness. They now allowed her to keep a candle burning in her room all night in case she needed light by which to compose verse. They also placed paper, a bottle of ink, and a quill on her nightstand; on cold nights, they made sure the fireplace in her quarters was kept burning. It is safe to assume that the Wheatley home was the only one in Boston where a slave greeted her masters in the morning with poems she had written during the night.

Phillis Wheatley's health continued to be poor, perhaps as a result of asthma or even tuberculosis. In many ways the Wheatleys treated her like a vulnerable and exotic flower. Whenever her condition became especially severe, Susannah Wheatley sent her to the country to rest and recover—again, hardly the kind of treatment received by the average slave in colonial New England.

One day, while Phillis was visiting at the home of another Boston family, the weather suddenly turned cold and damp. Fearing for the young woman's delicate health, Susannah Wheatley sent Prince to fetch her in the family carriage. When the carriage returned to the Wheatley mansion, Phillis was sitting up front in the driver's seat with Prince. Furious, Susannah Wheatley rebuked him for his "impudence" in seating Phillis with himself instead of inside the carriage, where a person of higher rank belonged.

A modern reader can only guess how Phillis Wheatley felt about this matter, but it is likely that she would have enjoyed forming some human attachments. In any case, on that cold and bleak day, Susannah Wheatley made it

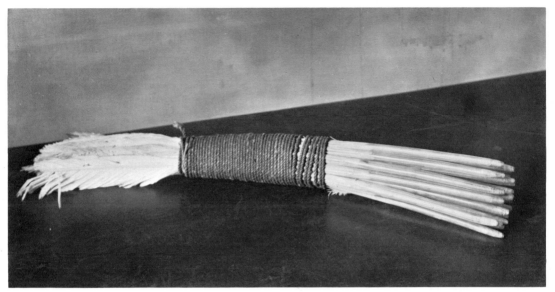

Goose-feather quills were essential equipment for an 18th-century writer. Their tips were sharpened with small blades known as penknives. Wheatley was kept well supplied with such tools.

clear that "her Phillis" was not to associate on friendly, equal terms with other blacks. Phillis Wheatley's writings offer no clue as to whether her opinion of herself was as high as that of her mistress.

She had one black woman friend, a fellow slave named Obour Tanner. Although there is no record of Wheatley and Tanner's first encounter, they had probably met in Newport, Rhode Island, where Tanner worked, and where the Wheatley family went for vacations. The two women had much in common: Both had been brought to America at about the same time, both had been acquired by families that educated them, both were deeply religious. Because Wheatley's mistress had strongly discouraged her from associating with other black people, Tanner was not only her best friend, but probably the only person of her own race she knew well.

The favored young woman was thus in a sort of limbo between two worlds, one black, one white. Although she was held to be superior to her fellow slaves, she herself remained a slave in the service of her masters. Her daily routine as a young domestic was not all arts and letters. Susannah Wheatley, according to Odell, "did not require or permit her services as a domestic, but she would sometimes allow her to polish a table or dust an apartment." She

Churchgoers watch in horror as a runaway slave is recovered by her cruel master. Lurid images like this one were often circulated by the abolitionist, or antislavery, movement.

Eunice Fitch was among the Bostonians who invited Wheatley to their homes. Ironically, it was a ship owned by Fitch's husband that had brought the young poet to America.

Prosperous Boston merchant Timothy Fitch made most of his money through the buying and selling of black Africans. Phillis Wheatley was named after one of his slave ships.

was also reported to have been assigned to "tending table" during dinner parties.

As Phillis Wheatley's talent continued to develop, Susannah Wheatley, almost as if she were a "stage mother," began to promote the young woman's career. She invited important Boston merchants, politicians, and clergymen to her home to behold the amazing "dark child from Africa." She also began to bring and send her to the homes of other upper-class Bostonians. Able to hold her own in conversations with learned men about literature, the Bible,

and other weighty subjects, Phillis Wheatley started to earn a reputation as a lively, even brilliant, young woman.

Through these visits, she met such influential people as Governor Thomas Hutchinson, Lieutenant Governor Andrew Oliver, and legislator John Hancock. To encourage her in her studies, some of these distinguished admirers provided her with books, expensive luxuries in colonial times.

In short, Phillis Wheatley was a social sensation. Wealthy and cultivated Bostonians were deeply impressed when they heard a young African

woman accurately reflect the thoughts and values of their white, Christian society. Susannah Wheatley became expert at showcasing the young woman's various gifts.

Despite her warm reception in the city's fashionable drawing rooms, Phillis Wheatley was always aware of the vast gulf between her hosts and herself. Even when she was ostensibly the guest of honor on such occasions, she would politely refuse a seat at the table. Instead she would ask for a side table that kept her at a respectful distance from her white admirers.

Reporting on one such event, Odell observed that the young poet "must have been painfully conscious of the feelings with which her unfortunate race were regarded.... Respecting even the prejudices of those who cour-

The Old South Meeting House, still standing in Boston, was the scene of Wheatley's baptism in 1771. Pious New Englanders allowed blacks in their churches, but only in segregated sections.

teously waived them in her favor, she . . . placed herself where she could certainly expect neither to give or receive offense."

An especially awkward moment for both guest and hosts occurred when Susannah Wheatley sent her protégée to visit Eunice Fitch and her daughters. Ironically, it was to this family that Phillis Wheatley owed her residence in America; Timothy Fitch, Eunice's husband, owned the *Phillis*—the very schooner that had carried the future poet across the Atlantic and into slavery.

The Fitch women were cordial to their visitor, but as teatime approached, the daughters grew visibly nervous. It was obvious that they were uncomfortable about sitting down to eat with a black servant, no matter how celebrated that servant might be. The young poet rose to depart, but Eunice Fitch insisted that she remain as the tea was poured. Wheatley stayed, but although the daughters were beguiled with her lively conversation, a hint of tension remained in the air.

If this was a victory for Phillis, it was a small one. Her accomplishments had earned her a place in white society, but it was clear that that place was not at the same table with the whites who applauded her.

Growing up in the Wheatley household, the young African woman absorbed Boston's Puritan culture and religion. She attended services at the Old South Meeting House, where she was introduced to the teachings of the "Great Awakening," a powerful religious revival movement that swept the colonies in the 18th century.

The Awakening was spread by clergymen who traveled through the country, hoping to revitalize what they saw as a flagging interest in religion. One of the movement's most influential preachers was an English evangelist named George Whitefield. He toured the colonies, holding open-air meetings that attracted enormous crowds at every stop.

Whitefield was an electrifying speaker, said to be capable of reducing his listeners to tears merely by saying the word "Mesopotamia." Samuel Johnson, the generally critical and sarcastic English writer, had said of Whitefield, "He would be followed by crowds were he to wear a nightcap in the pulpit, or were he to preach from a tree." Like the Awakening's other ministers, Whitefield taught that salvation was available to all; every human being, he said, had an equal chance to obtain God's grace.

This doctrine, which particularly appealed to the poor and oppressed, was a natural magnet for someone who could not even claim possession of her own person. Phillis Wheatley embraced it with all her heart, later basing much of her poetry on its ideas. Indi-

An Address to the Atheist. By P. Wheatley at the age of
14 years. — 1767

Muse! where shall I begin the spacious feild
To tell what curses unbeleif doth yeild?
Thou who dost daily feel his hand, and rod
Darest thou deny the Essence of a God!
If there's no heav'n, ah! whither wilt thou go,
Make thy Elysium in the shades below?
If there's no God from whom did all things Spring
He made the greatest and minutest Thing
Angelic ranks no less his Power display
Than the least mite scarce visible to Day
With vast astonishment my Soul is Struck
Have Reason's powers thy dark end breast forsook?
The Laws deep Graven by the hand of God.
Seal'd with Immanuel's all-redeeming blood:
This second point thy folly dares deny
On thy devoted head for vengeance cry —
Turn then I pray thee from the dangerous road
Rise from the dust and seek the mighty God.
His is bright truth without a dark disguise
And his are wisdom's all beholding Eyes:
With labour'd snares our Adversary great
Withholds from us the Kingdom and the seat
Bliss weeping waits thee, in her arms to fly
To her own regions of felicity —
Perhaps thy ignorance will ask us where?
Go to the Corner Stone he will declare.
Thy heart in unbeleif will harden'd grow
Tho' much indulg'd in vicious pleasure now —
Thou tak'st unusual means; the path forbear
Unkind to others to thyself severe
Methinks I see the consequence thou'rt blind
Thy unbeleif disturbs the peaceful Mind.

Phillis Wheatley was 14 years old when she wrote the poem, "An Address to the Atheist." Amazed by the young woman's poetry, Bostonians were also impressed by her graceful penmanship.

rectly, Whitefield himself would later have a strong influence on her life.

One of Wheatley's earliest poems, written when she was 14, reflected her newfound but powerful religious faith. Fifty-six lines long, "An Address to the Atheist" contains the following challenge to the unbeliever:

> Thou who dost daily feel his hand, and rod
> Darest thou deny the Essence of a God!
> If there's no heav'n, ah! whither wilt thou go . . . ?

Phillis Wheatley's passionate embrace of the faith of her masters had a profound influence on her character. She saw a world watched over by a righteous God in eternal struggle with the forces of Satan. It was the duty of each individual to overcome Satan's temptations and to throw himself at the feet of the Lord, singing his praises. Many natural human impulses were sinful, according to this creed, and many thoughts and yearnings impure.

Wheatley often expressed such beliefs. In a letter to Obour Tanner, written when she was about 17, she said, "Let us be mindful of our high calling, continually on our guard, lest our treacherous hearts should give the adversary an advantage over us. O! who can think without horror of the snares of the devil?"

The human heart might have been "treacherous," but Wheatley found intense comfort in the God she had been taught to worship. In another letter to Tanner, she wrote, "In [Christ's] crucifixion may be seen marvelous displays of grace and love, sufficient to draw and invite us to the rich and endless treasures of his mercy. Let us rejoice in and adore the wonders of God's infinite Love in bringing us from a land semblant of darkness itself."

By her early teenage years, Wheatley was already a poet as competent and talented as any in America. Her literary model was the celebrated English poet Alexander Pope, who had died 17 years before her arrival on the Boston docks. She imitated the form and classical imagery of Pope's translation of Homer's *Iliad*, but she was probably not familiar with his satirical poems, the work for which he is most admired today.

A Catholic in Protestant-dominated England, Pope had considered himself a member of an unjustly treated minority, much as Wheatley herself was. Pope, however, had been free to attack such injustice with the weapon of satire. Wheatley was not. Even if she had wanted to express bitterness about slavery in her poetry, she would not have dared. Tolerance in prerevolutionary America, even in relatively liberal Boston, only went so far.

The society in which Phillis Wheatley was growing up was a world filled with contradictions and paradoxes. She was a slave, but she was denied the company and companionship of

A 1774 engraving shows Death and Satan preparing to claim a sinner. To Wheatley and other deeply religious people of her time, the devil was a very real — and extremely frightening — presence.

her fellow servants. She was praised for her accomplishments, but she was often reminded that her blackness was at best unfortunate and at worst a curse. She was received by members of white society as a person of undeniable talent, but she would never be accepted as their social equal. And she was establishing a place for herself in a society that would soon be shattered by the convulsions of the American Revolution.

Alone in her room, she must have felt the stirrings of adolescence and young adulthood: the search for individual identity, the longing for human companionship, the desire to be welcomed into the human community, *any* human community.

In only seven years Phillis Wheatley had mastered a strange new language, fervently embraced a new religion, and proved that she had extraordinary gifts. She could look back with pride and confidence in her own abilities. Looking ahead, however, the view was cloudy. The Wheatleys were proud of her, but neither they nor she could regard the future with complete confidence.

Alexander Pope was celebrated for his savage wit and elegantly rhymed verse. Wheatley modeled her poetry after his, but her work was rarely bitter, and never humorous.

Crispus Attucks was the first black to die in the American struggle for independence. He was one of five civilians shot by British soldiers during the infamous Boston Massacre of 1770.

FOUR

An Expanding Fame

Phillis Wheatley's teenage years were a time of public excitement and private discovery. As her adopted nation moved toward war, she was expanding and refining her literary gift. Only a few years earlier, slave traders had been eager to sell her for a pittance; now she was poised on the brink of international fame.

Just as Wheatley's poetic voice was beginning to be heard, rumblings of the oncoming American Revolution began to fill the air. Many of the war's early confrontations erupted virtually on the Wheatleys' front doorstep. Phillis Wheatley had lived in Boston a little more than four years when she heard the first crackles of revolt.

In early 1765 the British Parliament passed the Stamp Act, a law that required the colonists to pay a tax on every newspaper, pamphlet, legal document, and deck of cards they printed. Stamp agents, American em-

ployees of the British government, sold the stamps and collected the fees. The law was despised by colonists from all walks of life.

In August 1765 a band of men who called themselves "Sons of Liberty" marched through the streets of Boston protesting the Stamp Act. Chanting "Liberty! Property, and no stamps!" they swarmed down King Street and turned onto Mackerel Lane, right in front of the Wheatley mansion.

Continuing to shout their slogan, the protesters attacked the newly built Stamp Office building, just down the street from the Wheatley home. They destroyed it, then rushed toward the house of stamp collector Andrew Oliver, an influential Bostonian whose path would later cross that of Phillis Wheatley. The rioters tore down Oliver's fence, smashed his windows, drank his wine, and built bonfires in front of his stately residence. Clearly,

Protesting the Stamp Act, Bostonians take to the streets in 1765. Imposed by the British, the notorious Stamp Act called for taxes on almost everything printed in the colonies.

the mood of the colonies was explosive. It was going to get worse.

A few days later, Boston mobs attacked the homes of men they considered pro-British "aristocrats." One of them was Lieutenant Governor Thomas Hutchinson who, although he had opposed the Stamp Act himself, was forced to watch as his elegant mansion was looted and destroyed by the protesters. Many Bostonians were appalled by these displays of rage and violence, but history was already on the move.

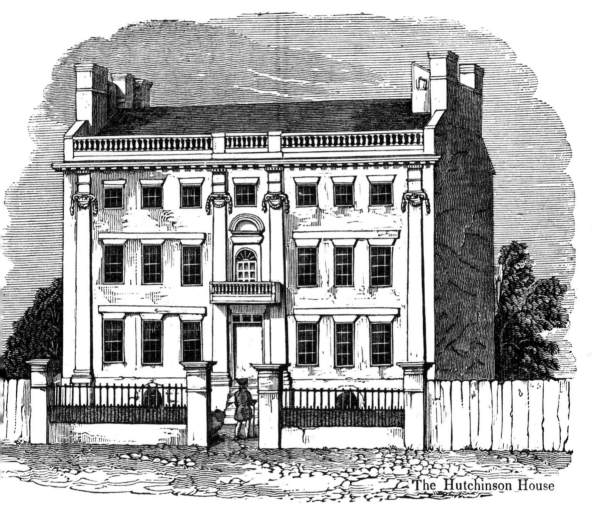

The stately home of Thomas Hutchinson was wrecked by anti-Stamp Act rioters in 1765. Bostonians officially censured the "horrid scene" — but offered its victim no compensation.

Through much of her adolescence, Wheatley had only to look out her front door to see that the impending conflict was coming closer by the day. In the fall of 1768, two regiments of British troops landed in Boston. Accompanied by artillery and drums, the red-coated soldiers marched confidently up King Street in a show of strength intended to impress the watching colonists.

The spectacle inspired Phillis Wheatley to compose a poem, "On the Arrival of the Ships of War, and Landing of the Troops." Unfortunately no copy

of these lines has survived, but we know from Wheatley poems inspired by other prerevolutionary events that she had strong pro-independence sympathies.

One such event occurred in 1770, not far from the Wheatley house. During a street-corner shouting match about British taxation, Christopher Snider, an 11-year-old boy, was shot and killed by a Tory (British sympathizer) named Ebenezer Richardson. After hearing of the incident, Wheatley wrote "On the death of Mr. Snider Murder'd by Richardson," in which she described the dead youth as "the first martyr for the cause"—a clear indication of which side she was on.

Eager to speed up colonial independence from Britain, American radicals were doing their best to whip colonial resentment of British troops into a fury. Largely through the circulation of *The Journal of Public Occurrences*, a weekly newspaper that contained exaggerated tales of British military drunkenness and brutality, the radicals had succeeded. Many Bostonians were eager to take on the "lobster-backs," as they called the British soldiers.

British ships enter Boston harbor in September 1768. The event prompted 15-year-old Phillis Wheatley to write a poem: "On the Arrival of the Ships of War, and Landing of the Troops."

A month after young Snider's death, they had their chance. On March 5, 1770, a violent confrontation, whose echoes would reverberate through history, took place near the Wheatleys' home. A restless group of men and boys had gathered at the customs house on King Street, where they began to hurl snowballs at a British sentry. He was joined by about 20 of his colleagues, who soon found themselves facing a mob of several hundred jeering, stone-throwing Bostonians. Acting without orders, one of the British soldiers suddenly opened fire. More shots rang out; within minutes, three Americans lay dead in the snow.

The first to fall was a middle-aged black man named Crispus Attucks. A former slave, Attucks had been working as a seaman since he had run away from his Massachusetts master 20 years earlier. The bloody incident, which the radicals quickly labeled "The Boston Massacre," ignited a storm of outrage throughout the colonies. The victims' funeral, the largest ever seen in Boston, drew thousands of grieving marchers.

Apparently deeply moved by the event, Phillis Wheatley wrote a poem about it, "On the Affray in King Street, on the Evening of the 5th of March, 1770." To the regret of literary scholars, nothing remains of this poem except its title.

Although she was absorbed by the rapidly unfolding political drama, Wheatley kept up with her studies, which now included geography, history, astronomy, and mythology as well as literature and Latin. She also continued to read the Bible and to attend services at the Old South Meeting House, the Congregational church where her mistress worshiped. It was here that George Whitefield, the spellbinding evangelist of the Great Awakening, preached a series of sermons in August 1770.

Whitefield had a powerful effect on everyone who heard him. Even Benjamin Franklin, known for both his skepticism and his thrift, was impressed by the magnetic clergyman. In his *Autobiography*, Franklin recalled the occasion when he had gone to hear Whitefield preach. He had "silently resolved," he said, that Whitefield "should get nothing from me." As he listened to the evangelist, however, he decided to contribute the pennies in his pocket to the collection plate. Hearing a little more, he determined to part with the three silver dollars he was carrying. Finally, said Franklin, Whitefield "finished so admirably, that I emptied my pocket wholly into the collectors' dish, gold and all."

The ministers of the Great Awakening taught that true Christianity meant love of one's fellow men—including "orphans, paupers, Indians, and slaves." While Whitefield and his col-

Taunted beyond endurance, British sentries open fire on a Boston mob in 1770. Known as the Boston Massacre, the confrontation strengthened anti-British sentiment among the colonists.

leagues did not specifically campaign against slavery, they insisted that people of all colors were spiritual equals. They introduced the idea that it was sinful for the white man to enslave his black brother, who also had an immortal soul.

Whitefield's American tour had been sponsored by a British noblewoman, Selina Hastings, countess of Huntingdon. Both very religious and very rich, Huntingdon employed dozens of chaplains, whom she sent around England, Wales, and the American colonies to encourage "backsliding" Christians to "return to the fold."

A month after Whitefield preached at the Old South Meeting House, the charismatic clergyman died suddenly at the age of 56. Because his message had touched Phillis Wheatley deeply, it is not surprising that his death inspired her to compose an elegy (a poem lamenting a death). The first words of its long, typically 18th-century title were "An Elegiac Poem on the

The 29th Regiment have already left us, and the 14th Regiment are following them, so that we expect the Town will soon be clear of all the Troops. The Wisdom and true Policy of his Majesty's Council and Col. Dalrymple the Commander appear in this Measure. Two Regiments in the midst of this populous City ; and the Inhabitants justly incensed : Those of the neighbouring Towns actually under Arms upon the first Report of the Massacre, and the Signal only wanting to bring in a few Hours to the Gates of this City many Thousands of our brave Brethren in the Country, deeply affected with our Distresses, and to whom we are greatly obliged on this Occasion—No one knows where this would have ended, and what important Consequences even to the whole British Empire might have followed, which our Moderation & Loyalty upon so trying an Occasion, and our Faith in the Commander's Assurances have happily prevented.

Last Thursday, agreeable to a general Request of the Inhabitants, and by the Consent of Parents and Friends, were carried to their *Grave* in Succession, the Bodies of *Samuel Gray, Samuel Maverick, James Caldwell,* and *Crispus Attucks,* the unhappy Victims who fell in the bloody Massacre of the Monday Evening preceeding !

On this Occasion most of the Shops in Town were shut, all the Bells were ordered to toll a solemn Peal, as were also those in the neighboring Towns of Charlestown Roxbury, &c. The Procession began to move between the Hours of 4 and 5 in the Afternoon ; two of the unfortunate Sufferers, viz. Mess. *James Caldwell* and *Crispus Attucks,* who were Strangers, borne from Faneuil-Hall, attended by a numerous Train of Persons of all Ranks ; and the other two, viz. Mr. *Samuel Gray,* from the House of Mr. Benjamin Gray, (his Brother) on the North-side the Exchange, and Mr. *Maverick,* from the House of his distressed Mother Mrs. *Mary Maverick,* in Union-Street, each followed by their respective Relations and Friends : The several Hearses forming a Junction in King-Street, the Theatre of that inhuman Tragedy ! proceeded from thence thro' the Main-Street, lengthened by an immense Concourse of People, so numerous as to be obliged to follow in Ranks of six, and brought up by a long Train of Carriages belonging to the principal Gentry of the Town. The Bodies were deposited in one Vault in the middle Burying-ground : The aggravated Circumstances of their Death, the Distress and Sorrow visible in every Countenance, together with the peculiar Solemnity with which the whole Funeral was conducted, surpass Description.

The image of coffins, each marked with the initials of a man killed in the Boston Massacre, was ideal propaganda for radicals who wanted immediate war with the British.

Death of the celebrated Divine, and eminent Servant of Jesus Christ, the late Reverend, and pious George Whitefield, Chaplain to Right Honourable the Countess of Huntingdon, &c, &c, Who made his exit from this transitory State, to dwell in the Celestial Realms of Bliss, on Lord's Day, 30th of September, 1770.''

The elegy, identified as "a Condolatory Address to His truly noble Benefactoress the pious Lady Huntingdon," carried the following information about its author: "By Phillis, a Servant Girl of 17 Years of Age, belonging to Mr. J. Wheatley, of Boston:—and has been but 9 years in this Country from Africa." The first major work of this young black woman, then, was a tribute to a middle-aged white man. The elegy begins with these lines:

Hail, happy saint, on thine immortal
throne,
Possest of glory, life and bliss unknown;
We hear no more the music of thy
tongue. . . .

Whitefield, according to the elegy, had made a point of urging blacks to accept Christ:

"Take him, ye Africans, he longs for you,
Impartial Saviour is his title due;
Washed in the fountain of redeeming
blood,
You shall be sons and kings, and Priests
to God."

Wheatley's elegy for Whitefield was published in pamphlet form and as a broadside (handbill) in Boston, Philadelphia, New York, and Newport, Rhode Island. Partly because the clergyman had been so well known and so hugely popular, the poem scored a resounding success, transforming Wheatley from a local phenomenon into a poet celebrated throughout the colonies. And because the clergyman had been the personal emissary of the countess of Huntingdon, it was almost inevitable that the poem would carry its author's fame across the ocean. Hastings's favorable reaction to the poem would prove very important to Wheatley.

About a year after Whitefield's death, in August 1772, Phillis Wheatley was formally accepted as a member of the Old South Meeting House. Despite her local renown, she was baptized, according to a later report in the *Boston Daily Advertiser*, "under the simple and unpretending name of Phillis, the servant of Mr. Wheatley, with no surname whatever."

If the young woman resented being so identified, she left no record of it. She wrote, in fact, a poem expressing joy in her introduction to the New World and the Christian religion. This poem, "On Being Brought from Africa to America," opens with the line, "'Twas mercy brought me from my pagan land." The last lines of the verse

British preacher George Whitefield invokes a blessing on his flock. The death of the evangelist, whose sermons had thrilled Wheatley, inspired her to write one of her most popular poems.

are "Remember, Christians, Negros black as Cain/ May be refined, and join the angelic train."

After the success of the Whitefield elegy, Susannah Wheatley decided it was time to collect some of her protégée's poems in a book. Getting it published, however, proved difficult. Then as now, most printers were willing to publish only books from which they expected to make a profit. They required prospective authors to provide

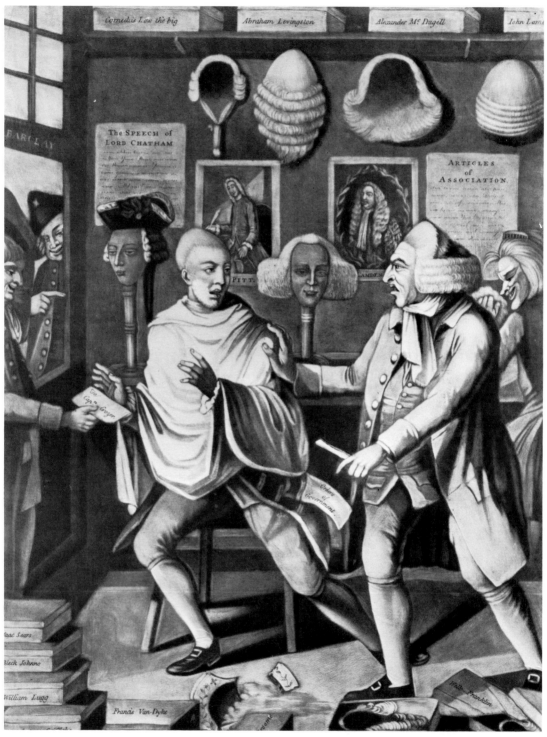

The caption accompanying this political cartoon of 1775 told patriotic American barbers how to deal with red-coated customers: "Half shave them first, then send 'em home."

the names of at least 300 people who guaranteed to buy their books.

With that in mind, in the spring of 1772 Susannah Wheatley ran a series of advertisements in the *Boston Censor*. Seeking sponsors, she listed the titles of the 28 Wheatley poems she wanted to include in the book. Because the young poet was already admired throughout New England, and because many of her poems reflected the American cause, Susannah Wheatley undoubtedly expected an enthusiastic response from the Boston community.

Many educated New Englanders were supportive of blacks' efforts to improve their fortunes, and many favored the eventual abolition of slavery. Nevertheless, few of these upper-class whites felt comfortable about admitting to the world that their sentiments could be expressed by a black woman slave. Susannah Wheatley soon discovered that not enough Bostonians were willing to put their names, let alone their money, behind such an admission. Without an adequate number of subscribers, no publisher would accept the book.

Despite this setback, Phillis Wheatley continued to acquire important allies. When William Legge, the earl of Dartmouth (after whom Dartmouth College is named), was appointed secretary of state for North America, Wheatley sent him a congratulatory letter and a poem.

A British official who had argued against the hated Stamp Act, Legge was regarded as a friend of the colonies. He had also been a friend of Whitefield and was a member of the countess of Huntingdon's religious circle; Wheatley must have felt confident that he would be receptive to unconventional ideas. In any case, the poem she sent him is the most uncharacteristically frank of all her surviving work.

In it, Wheatley makes her only specific reference to her kidnapping and enslavement and explains why her condition as an African slave makes her a particular partisan of freedom. The poem includes the following lines:

> Should you, my lord, while you peruse
> my song,
> Wonder from whence my love of
> freedom sprung,
> Whence flow these wishes for the
> common good,
> By feeling hearts alone best
> understood,—
> I, young in life, by seeming cruel fate
> Was snatch'd from Afric's fancied happy
> seat:
> What pangs excruciating must molest,
> What sorrows labour in my parent's
> breast?
> Steeled was that soul and by no misery
> moved,
> That from a father seized his babe
> beloved:
> Such, such my case. And can I then but
> pray
> Others may never feel tyrannic sway?

These are unusually personal lines for an 18th-century poem. Poets of

Wheatley's era were expected to express ordinary, even conventional, reactions to public events. Indeed, most 18th-century poems are "occasional"—formal, stylized responses to specific public occasions such as births, deaths, and marriages. Readers of the 18th century expected their poets to be sincere and elegant in style, not dramatic or deeply emotional.

In the Dartmouth poem, Wheatley comes as close as a proper 18th-century poet could to exposing her most deeply felt memories and desires. The phrase "*seeming* cruel fate" implies a belief that her relocation to America was for the best; similarly, "Afric's *fancied* happy seat" suggests that she did not regard Africa as an ideal place.

Nevertheless, Wheatley uses fairly blunt language about the *manner* in which she was removed from her homeland and sold into bondage. She declares her love for freedom, equates slavery with tyranny, and voices the hope that no other human being be made to endure its suffering. Phillis Wheatley was 19 years old when she wrote this poem, which came perilously close to her society's limits of acceptability.

History contains no record of Dartmouth's reaction to Wheatley's poem. His sentiments about her theme, however, were made clear three years after she wrote to him. Commenting in 1775 about the growing New England op-

William Legge, the earl of Dartmouth, was a follower of "Great Awakening" preacher George Whitefield. Unlike that clergyman, however, Dartmouth regarded the slave trade as "beneficial."

position to slavery, he said, "We cannot allow the Colonies to check or to discourage in any degree a traffic so beneficial to the nation." Dartmouth may have admired Wheatley's poetry, but he obviously did not embrace her ideas about slavery.

Susannah Wheatley was disappointed by Boston's unwillingness to support her protégée's book, but she was not defeated. She decided that even if she could not get the book published in America, she might find a printer in London who would accept the job. That would be a real triumph; Boston, after all, was only a provincial capital, but London was one of the hubs of Western culture.

As the first step in her new campaign, she spoke to Robert Calef, skipper of the Wheatley schooner *London*. Calef was preparing to sail for England; when he got there, said Susannah Wheatley, she would appreciate his looking around for a possible printer for her protégée's book.

When he arrived in the British capital, the obliging sea captain began to make inquiries. He was soon directed to Archibald Bell, an obscure printer of religious works. Bell was apparently impressed with Phillis Wheatley's poetry, but he found it hard to believe it had been written by a black slave. He finally agreed to publish it, but only on one condition: that Calef provide proof that the poet was the person the skipper said she was.

When the captain brought this information back to Susannah Wheatley, she went to work at once. Before long, she had persuaded 18 prominent Bostonians to sign a document confirming her protégée's identity. Among the distinguished signers were the royal governor of the Massachusetts colony,

Thomas Hutchinson; future Massachusetts governor James Bowdoin; and John Hancock, the man who would go down in history for his large, bold signature on the Declaration of Independence. The last of the witnesses signed himself, "Mr. John Wheatley, her master."

When Phillis Wheatley's book finally appeared in print, it would include the Boston statement. Addressed "To the Publick," the document guaranteed that the poems in the book had been "written by Phillis, a young Negro girl, who was but a few years since, brought an uncultivated barbarian, from Africa, and has ever since been, and now is, under the disadvantage of serving as a slave in a family in this town."

Because the book was going to be published in England, Susannah Wheatley shrewdly suggested that certain poems be omitted. Among them were such pro-independence verses as "On the Arrival of the Ships of War, and Landing of the Troops" and "On the Affray in King Street, on the Evening of the 5th of March, 1770." Unfortunately, these poems were so well concealed that they have been lost to modern scholars.

By now confident that the book would be published, both Phillis Wheatley and her master wrote prefaces for it. Describing herself, the poet said, "As to the disadvantages she has laboured under, with regard to learn-

Thomas Hutchinson, one of those who signed a document confirming Wheatley's authorship, faced ongoing harassment for his support of British authority. In 1774, he fled to safety in England.

ing, nothing needs to be offered, as her Master's letter in the following page will sufficiently show the difficulties in this respect she has had to encounter."

John Wheatley's preface pointed out that the young woman "in 16 months time from her arrival, attained the English language, to which she was an utter stranger before, to such a degree as to read any of the most difficult parts of the Sacred Writings, to the great astonishment of all who heard her."

When Calef set sail for England on November 19, 1772, he carried a packet from Susannah Wheatley. Addressed to publisher Archibald Bell, it contained the document attesting to Phillis Wheatley's authorship, both prefaces, and a manuscript copy of 39 poems.

With the manuscript completed and a publisher ready to print it, the forthcoming book lacked only the name of the person to whom it would be dedicated. Dedications were important in the book trade of the 18th century; the name of an important person lent a book prestige and was likely to increase sales substantially. Susannah Wheatley knew that the countess of Huntingdon had been pleased by the elegy to her favorite chaplain, George Whitefield. Huntingdon, with her vast fortune and widespread religious and literary contacts, would be the perfect choice. But before the book could be dedicated to her, her permission would have to be obtained.

Susannah Wheatley instructed Bell to send the manuscript to Huntingdon along with a letter asking if it might be dedicated to her. Bell took it a step further. He brought the poems to the countess and read them to her himself.

He must have been an effective reader; in early 1773, Calef sent Susannah Wheatley a letter reporting that the countess was "fond" of having the book dedicated to her and wanted "Phillis' picture in the frontispiece." The captain said he thought such a portrait would greatly help the sales of the book.

Back in Boston, Phillis Wheatley sat for her portrait. Historians believe it was painted by Scipio Moorhead, a black slave who belonged to a Wheatley family friend, Presbyterian minister John Moorhead. No record of the portrait painter's identity has been found, but when Wheatley's book was published, it contained a poem called "To S. M., a Young African Painter," indicating that she was familiar with Scipio Moorhead and his work.

The portrait—the only one of Wheatley known to exist—shows a slender, large-eyed woman seated at a desk. She is wearing a white, ruffled cap and writing with a quill pen. An engraving made from this painting would appear in Phillis Wheatley's book; another would be hung in a place of honor over the Wheatleys' living-room fireplace.

Apparently, the portrait was a good

The countess of Huntingdon was rich, devout, and highly influential. Impressed by Phillis Wheatley's elegy to George Whitefield, she gave the young poet important public support.

likeness. A visitor to the Wheatleys' house reported that Susannah Wheatley often proudly pointed out her protégée's picture. "See!" she would say, "Look at my Phillis! Does she not seem as though she would speak to me?"

Soliciting subscribers for Phillis Wheatley's upcoming book, Susannah Wheatley placed advertisements in several Boston newspapers. As well as drumming up business, she was telling all Boston that the talents of "her Phillis" had been recognized by the literary establishment of London. Born in Africa and raised in slavery, this young black woman was about to make her mark on a world run by free white men.

Eager to help her career, Wheatley's English friends wanted to present her to King George III, pictured here. The poet, however, was called home before the royal interview could take place.

FIVE

A Triumphant Voyage

As the publication date of Phillis Wheatley's book approached, British interest in the poet and her work increased. The London literary establishment was intrigued by this curious new phenomenon: a young, female African slave who not only wrote poetry, but whose verses were as good as any "civilized" poet's.

In the spring of 1773, the Wheatleys' son, Nathaniel, was preparing to sail to England on family business. At the same time, the Wheatleys' doctor suggested that an ocean voyage might improve Phillis Wheatley's increasingly fragile health.

Despite the growing revolutionary fervor in Boston and other colonial capitals, London was still the cultural center of the English-speaking world. Concerned about the well-being of "her Phillis," and aware that a visit to the British capital could give the poet's career a significant boost, Susannah Wheatley decided to send her to London with Nathaniel.

On April 30, 1773, she wrote to the countess of Huntingdon to announce her protégée's forthcoming voyage. She said she had instructed the young poet "to act wholly under the direction of your Ladyship," adding that she had "given her money to buy what you think most proper for her" in the way of clothes. Her gifted servant, said Susannah Wheatley, "should be dress'd plain."

Huntingdon never took Phillis Wheatley shopping, but after she learned of the unusual young woman's projected trip to England, she spread the news among her friends in British literary and social circles. Meanwhile, Susannah Wheatley was busy sending notices to New England, New York, and Pennsylvania newspapers, announcing the imminent departure for London of this "extraordinary Negro poet."

Watched by their approving parents, young British aristocrats demonstrate their dancing skills. Wheatley was welcomed into many prominent families when she visited England in 1773.

Phillis Wheatley's travel plans were soon a topic of conversation on both sides of the Atlantic.

For her part, the poet composed 12 stanzas, entitled "A Farewell to America." Susannah Wheatley arranged to have the poem, which was addressed to "Mrs. S. W.," published in several newspapers. Typical of the work's emotional sensibilities and suggestive of the poet's feeling for her mistress were the following lines:

> Susannah mourns, nor can I bear
> To see the crystal shower,
> Or mark the tender falling tear,
> At sad departure's hour.

Phillis Wheatley sailed for England on May 8, 1773. This transatlantic crossing was a far cry from the voyage that had brought her to America a dozen years earlier. Then she had been a helpless child, imprisoned by harsh strangers and destined to be sold in the marketplace. Now 20 years old, she was a recognized poet, escorted by a prosperous businessman and awaited by many prominent Londoners.

Susannah Wheatley's efforts to promote her protégée did not end when the schooner *London* left Boston harbor with her son and the poet aboard. She was, in fact, busier than ever. Eager to keep Phillis Wheatley in the public eye, she mailed a copy of "A Farewell to America" to the editor of the *London Chronicle.*

Along with the poem, she sent the editor a letter about "the extraordinary Negro girl here, who has by her own application, unassisted by others, cultivated her natural talents for poetry in such a manner as to write several pieces which (all circumstances considered) have great merit." The *Chronicle* printed both the slave's poem and her mistress's letter. The Wheatley bandwagon was rolling on.

When the young poet arrived in London, she found herself something of a celebrity, even though her book had not yet been published. She plunged into a hectic schedule of social and literary engagements and met many celebrities. One of them was the earl of Dartmouth, the colonial secretary to whom she had earlier addressed her poem about being a slave. Another was Benjamin Franklin, in London as the colonial agent for Pennsylvania.

Writing to Obour Tanner about her stay in London, Wheatley talked about "the friends I found there among the nobility and gentry." In her characteristically modest tone, she added, "Their benevolent conduct towards me, the unexpected and unmerited civility and complaisance [graciousness] with which I was treated by all, fills me with astonishment." In some of Lon-

Wheatley acquired one of her most treasured possessions during her visit to London: a copy of Paradise Lost, *a long epic poem by the great 17th-century British poet, John Milton.*

don's more exclusive circles, Phillis Wheatley was the talk of the town.

The respect and honor with which white London society received its black American visitor reached a high point when the city's lord mayor presented her with a valuable edition of John Milton's *Paradise Lost.* The famed English poet was one of Wheatley's favorites.

As soon as she arrived in England,

When American statesman, scientist, and philosopher Benjamin Franklin (pictured here) met Phillis Wheatley in London, the two probably discussed George Whitefield, whom both had admired.

Wheatley had written a letter to the countess of Huntingdon. Dated June 27, 1773, it said, "It is with pleasure that I acquaint your ladyship of my safe arrival in London after a fine passage of five weeks in the Ship London with my young master. . . . I should think myself very happy in seeing your ladyship."

Huntingdon promptly responded by inviting the poet and her "young master" to visit her at her estate in South Wales. Pleased by the Englishwoman's offer of hospitality, the Americans made plans for the journey. Then an urgent message arrived from home: Susannah Wheatley's health was failing rapidly. She wanted her protégée to come back to Boston immediately.

The poet was bitterly disappointed, but she had no choice. On July 17, she sent another letter to Huntingdon. "I rec'd with mixed sensations of pleasure and disappointment your Ladyship's message," she wrote. "Am sorry to acquaint your Ladyship that the ship is certainly to sail next Thursday [on] which I must return to America. I long to see my friend there, [but I am] extremely reluctant to go without having first seen your Ladyship."

In her biography of Wheatley, Margaretta Odell noted that the poet's visit occurred in the summer, when the king and queen were away from London. She reported that Wheatley was "urgently pressed by her distinguished friends to remain until the court re-turned to St. James's, that she might be presented to the young monarch, George III." Such an introduction would have been both exciting and beneficial to Wheatley's writing career, but it was not to be.

On July 26, 1773, less than a month after she had arrived in England, Phillis Wheatley reboarded the *London* and sailed for Boston. Nathaniel, who had become engaged to marry the daughter of a wealthy London merchant, stayed behind to prepare for his upcoming wedding.

The shortened visit meant a double loss for the poet. First, she never met with Huntingdon, her strongest supporter in England and a woman she much admired. Second, she was not present for what might have been the greatest event of her life: the long-awaited London publication of her book.

That event would be a milestone in literary history. Although more than 150 years had passed since the Pilgrims first landed in Massachusetts, few colonial women considered themselves writers. Wheatley's volume, *Poems on Various Subjects, Religious and Moral*, was, in fact, only the second book published by an American woman. (The first had been a volume of poetry by British-born colonist Anne Bradstreet, published in London in 1650.) Wheatley's book was, furthermore, the first ever published by an American black

PHILLIS WHEATLEY, NEGRO SERVANT to Mr. JOHN WHEATLEY, of BOSTON.

Publiſhed according to Act of Parliament, Sept. 1, 1773 by Arch.d Bell.
Bookſeller N.o 8 near the Saracens Head Aldgate.

P O E M S

O N

VARIOUS SUBJECTS,

RELIGIOUS AND MORAL.

B Y

PHILLIS WHEATLEY,

NEGRO SERVANT to Mr. JOHN WHEATLEY, of BOSTON, in NEW ENGLAND.

L O N D O N:
Printed for A. BELL, Bookſeller, Aldgate; and ſold by Meſſrs. COX and BERRY, King-Street, *BOSTON.*

M DCC LXXIII.

Wheatley's first — and only — book, Poems on Various Subjects, Religious and Moral, *was published in London on September 1, 1773. It included "an elegant engraving" of its author.*

person of either sex. Her achievement was especially noteworthy in light of her youth.

It is not hard to imagine how the young poet would have felt had she been allowed to stay in London to witness the enthusiastic reception her work would receive. Nevertheless, she must have known she had achieved a rare triumph.

She must also have savored vivid memories of her sojourn in England and of her generous reception there. As a black writer in a white world, she would always be an oddity. Londoners, however, had treated her more like an equal than Americans ever had. In fact, the question of her status as a slave would soon become a topic of intense discussion among British critics, intellectuals, and clergymen.

As the schooner *London* plowed

slowly across the Atlantic, literary events were moving rapidly in the city of London. Probably aware that he had a profitable property on his hands, publisher Archibald Bell began an extensive publicity campaign. Before publication, he ran a series of newspaper advertisements announcing the imminent release of an important book, "Written by PHILLIS, A Negro Servant to Mr. Wheatley, of Boston in New England."

In September 1773 the first copies rolled off the press, and Bell pulled out all the stops. In each of London's many daily newspapers, he placed lengthy, effusive notices about the book. He emphasized its dedication to Huntingdon, included the signed statement attesting to Wheatley's authorship, and noted that the volume was "Adorned with an Elegant Engraving of the Author." The book was, according to Bell's breathless announcements, "perhaps one of the greatest instances of pure, unassisted genius, that the world ever produced."

Wheatley's poems received highly complimentary reviews in at least a dozen English and Scottish newspapers, many of which included excerpts from the poems. As well as praising the book, however, several reviewers also criticized Boston's white citizens, including the Wheatleys, for the hypocrisy of honoring the poet while keeping her in slavery.

"The people of Boston," said one critic, "boast themselves chiefly on their principles of liberty. One such act as the purchase of [Phillis Wheatley's] freedom would, in our opinion, have done more honour than hanging a thousand trees with ribbons and emblems."

Perhaps the Wheatleys were stung by British criticism of the poet's slave status, or perhaps they had already been planning to free her. Whatever their reasons, they released Phillis Wheatley from slavery not long after she returned from England. Surprisingly, no record remains, either in the poet's correspondence or in family records, of the exact date of her manumission (liberation).

After she was freed, the young woman's life remained much the same at first—except that now she was responsible for her own economic wellbeing. The sales of her book thus took on a new importance. She waited anxiously for the arrival of the first shipment of 300 copies so she could begin selling them. As it turned out, Bell was so busy filling orders in London that he did not send the books to Boston until early 1774.

The poet continued to live with the Wheatleys, devoting much of her time and energy to caring for her gravely ill mistress. When she had time, she continued to write; she also made frequent visits to the homes of prominent Bos-

An early 19th-century English children's book shows youngsters petitioning for abolition of the slave trade. The British Empire outlawed slavery in 1834; the United States, 29 years later.

tonians who wanted to hear about her London trip.

On October 30, 1773, the poet wrote a letter to her friend Obour Tanner, by now also a free woman. Wheatley "humbly hoped," she said, that the visit to England would have "the happy effect of lessening me in my own esteem." Like all her letters, this one was filled with religious sentiments. "The God of the seas and dry land," she said, "has graciously brought me home in safety. Join with me in thanks to him for so great a mercy."

Wheatley covered several other subjects in this letter. She gave Tanner the latest news about Susannah Wheatley: "My mistress has been very sick above 14 weeks, and confined to her bed the whole time, but is I hope somewhat better now." She solicited her friend's aid in selling her book, asking her to "use your influence to get subscriptions, as it is for my benefit."

She also mentioned the bearer of the letter, a note of special interest in light of later developments in Wheatley's life. "The young man by whom this is handed you," she said, "seems to me to be a very clever man, knows you very well, and is very complaisant and agreeable." The young man's name was John Peters; he would also come to know Phillis Wheatley very well.

In early 1774, the American campaign on behalf of Wheatley's book finally got under way. Notices announcing its availability appeared in the *Boston Gazette and Journal* and the *Gazette and Boston Weekly News Letter* in January and February.

Despite her reserved nature, Phillis Wheatley had good business instincts. She knew that as a free woman she could no longer expect the Wheatleys to manage her life; she would have to generate sales of the book herself. She worked at it diligently among her New England friends and admirers.

One of these friends was Sampson Occom, a 41-year-old Mohegan Indian who had become a Christian missionary. On February 11, 1774, Wheatley wrote the Indian clergyman a remarkable letter. In it, she attacked the hypocrisy of a white Christian society that enslaved its fellow human beings. The tone of the letter is uncharacteristically sharp, perhaps indicating that Wheatley had gained new self-confidence during her first few months of freedom.

Sampson Occom, a well-known missionary and abolitionist, received a surprisingly outspoken letter from Wheatley in 1774; in it, she denounced slaveholding Christians as hypocrites.

Here was a new Phillis Wheatley, an individual who was neither humble nor accommodating, a black woman giving heartfelt testimony to what may well have been the most crucial issue of her existence. The theme of injustice never made a strong appearance in Wheatley's poetry, but if the letter to Occom is any evidence, it was never far from her heart.

"In every human breast, God has implanted a principle, which we call love of freedom; it is impatient of oppression, and pants for deliverance," she wrote. "I will assert that the same principle lives in us." The letter went on to wish for God's help in bringing about

A letter from Wheatley to Obour Tanner, written on March 21, 1774, reveals sad news. "I have lately met with a great trial," wrote the poet, "in the death of my mistress."

JOIN or DIE

This graphic plea for solidarity — the work of Benjamin Franklin — shows the colonies as parts of a snake that must "join or die." Coming from the snake's head are the words "Unite and conquer."

the downfall of "those whose avarice impels them to countenance and help forward the calamities of their fellow creatures."

She hoped for such help, she said, not to hurt those "whose words and actions are so diametrically opposite," but "to convince them of the strange absurdity of their conduct." She insisted that it did not "require the penetration of a philosopher" to understand that the "cry for liberty" could not coexist with the "disposition for the exercise of oppressive power over others."

Wheatley's words may not seem daring to modern readers. Spoken by a black woman in the 18th century, however, they were almost revolutionary. Her bold indictment of slavery and hypocrisy was first published on March 11, 1774, in the *Connecticut Gazette*, probably at Occom's instigation. During the next few weeks, it was reprinted in many other New England newspapers, which suggests that Phillis Wheatley's argument found a receptive audience in a large number of American homes.

A week before her letter to Occom appeared in print, Wheatley suffered a painful loss. Susannah Wheatley, her lifelong sponsor, mentor, and friend, died at the age of 65 on March 3, 1774.

"Let us imagine the loss of a parent, sister or brother," she wrote to Obour Tanner. "The tenderness of all these was united in her. I was a poor little outcast and stranger when she took me in; not only into her house, but I presently became a sharer in her most tender affections. I was treated by her more like her child than her servant."

Phillis Wheatley told Tanner that her mistress's faith in heaven had comforted her survivors. She "departed," said the poet, "in inexpressible rapture, earnest longings, and impatient thirstings for the upper courts of the Lord."

Phillis Wheatley's life was undergoing rapid and drastic changes. At the age of 21 she was a free woman, but she had lost the person who had done the most to support and encourage her. She had become a celebrated poet, but the society in which she had achieved her triumph was on the brink of a tremendous upheaval.

In May 1774, Wheatley finally received the 300 copies of her book for which she had been impatiently waiting. It was fortunate that the books, which quickly found eager buyers, arrived when they did; if Bell had waited even a few weeks longer to send them

Throwing — literally — a party in Boston harbor, Patriots heave British-owned tea overboard in late 1773. This act of rebellion, known as the Boston Tea Party, brought the outbreak of war closer.

THIS DAY IS PUBLISHED,
Adorn'd with an elegant Engraving of the Author
[Price 3s. 4d. L. M. Bud]
POEMS,
On various fubj&ts.——Religious and Moral.
By PHILLIS WHEATLEY,
A Negro Girl.
Sold by Mefs'rs COX & BERRY,
At their Store in King Street, Bofton.
N. B. The Subfcribers are requefted to apply for
their Copies.

An advertisement in The Boston Gazette *announces the availability of Wheatley's* Poems. *Copies of the book arrived in Boston in May 1774, eight months after its publication in London.*

from London, they might never have reached their author. On June 1, 1774, the British threw a blockade around Boston harbor, preventing the passage of ships in and out of the city.

The blockade was part of a series of repressive measures called the "Intolerable Acts." These laws were passed by the British Parliament in retaliation for a colonial gesture of defiance known as the Boston Tea Party. Infuriated by British taxes that they considered wholly unjust, a band of American radicals had staged the spectacular drama on the evening of December 16, 1773.

As a huge crowd of Bostonians cheered, about 150 "Sons of Liberty" had stormed aboard two British merchant ships moored in the harbor. The men, disguised as Indians, had seized the ships' cargo, 342 chests of tea, and pitched it into the water. The Bostonians' refusal to pay for the destroyed tea sparked the blockade of the city.

Boston's leading citizens—the same people who had joined to applaud the emergence of an African slave poet—

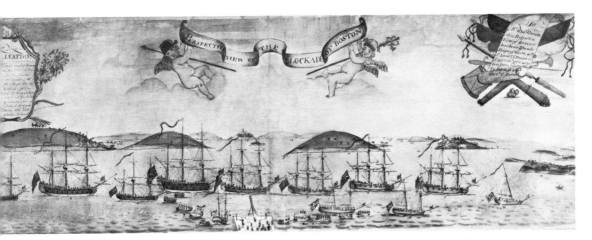

The British blockade of Boston, enacted after the celebrated Boston Tea Party, effectively isolated the city from the rest of the world. It went into effect on June 1, 1774.

now found themselves in opposing political camps. Two of the men who had signed the document confirming Phillis Wheatley's authorship became particularly bitter adversaries. John Hancock was firmly allied with the radicals who sought independence from England; Governor Thomas Hutchinson would soon be driven into exile as an enemy of the Patriots' cause.

A year after Susannah Wheatley's death, the American Revolution was under way. No American—not even a gentle, religious poet recently freed from slavery—would escape the war's fiery blast.

George Washington arrives in Cambridge to take command of the Continental army on July 2, 1775. Eight months later, the general received Phillis Wheatley at his headquarters.

SIX

Freedom and War

In the summer of 1774, Phillis Wheatley received a letter from John Thornton, a wealthy member of the countess of Huntingdon's religious circle. Thornton, who had met the poet when she visited London the year before, offered to take over Susannah Wheatley's role as her patron and spiritual mentor. He also said he would be happy to sponsor her as a Christian missionary in Africa.

Phillis Wheatley was faced with mounting financial pressures. Thornton's offer was therefore attractive, but she had no desire to resume her status as someone's protégée. She politely declined his offer of assistance and gently but decisively rejected his invitation to return to Africa.

As if on cue, a merchant ship slipped through the British blockade, delivering another shipment of books to Wheatley. She quickly placed advertisements in the *Boston Evening Post* and *Advertiser*. Unlike her earlier notices, these did not describe the poems as the work of a slave, but as the writings of "Phillis Wheatley, A Negro Girl, Printed for the Benefit of the Author."

As Wheatley was planning her new sales campaign, military and political events were unfolding that would profoundly affect her, her fellow Bostonians, and every other resident of the American colonies.

By early 1775, Boston was occupied by almost 5,000 British soldiers. Under the Quartering Act—one of the "Intolerable Acts" passed by Parliament in 1774—Bostonians were forced to provide accommodations in their homes for the British troops. Evidence indicates that two young British naval officers were quartered in the Wheatley mansion. Both officers had served in Africa, and it is likely that they talked to Phillis Wheatley about their experiences in her homeland. In 1775, she wrote a poem called "Reply," which may have been inspired by such conversations. The poem is the first recorded celebration of an African heritage by a black American. Among its lines are these:

> Charmed with thy painting, how my
>   bosom burns!
> And pleasing Gambia on my soul
>   returns,
> With native grace in spring's luxuriant
>   reign,
> Smiles the gay mead, and Eden blooms
>   again,
> The various bower, the tuneful flowing
>   stream,
> The soft retreats, the lovers' golden
>   dream,
> Her soil spontaneous, yields exhaustless
>   stores;
> For Phoebus revels on her verdant
>   shores.
> Whose flowery births, a fragrant train
>   appear,
> And crown the youth throughout the
>   smiling year.
> There, as in Britain's favour'd isle,
>   behold
> The bending harvest ripens into gold!
> Just are thy views of Afric's blissful
>   plain,
> On the warm limits of the land and
>   main.

This loving tribute to Africa contrasts dramatically with lines written earlier in her career, when she had referred to Africa as "my pagan land." She had once regarded her passage from Africa to the New World as a journey from darkness into light; now she was looking back at Africa with affection and pride. Clearly, her attitude toward her birthplace had undergone an evolution. If her heritage had ever been a source of shame, it was no longer.

Although "Reply" reveals an important shift in the poet's feelings, its style was not in tune with the demands of revolutionary times. Wheatley's approach was calm and classical; the conflict sweeping across the colonies called for lines written on a drumhead, ringing with defiance.

Boston was seething with tension in early 1775. The city was full of red-coated British troops, its harbor packed with heavily armed British warships. Fights among soldiers and civilians were common, and rumors of new British restraints circulated everywhere. Most often repeated was the prediction that General Thomas Gage, commander of British forces in Boston, would move to establish martial (military) law in the surrounding countryside.

Preparing to resist such an effort, the colonists had spent the winter collecting arms and training minutemen—militia who could go into action "at a minute's notice." New England was a powder keg, and on April 18, Gage released the spark that ignited it.

When he received word that the colonists had stockpiled a large supply of munitions at Concord, a few miles outside Boston, Gage dispatched 1,000 redcoats to disarm the rebellious

British troops open fire on minutemen at Lexington, Massachusetts, on April 19, 1775. Eight Americans were killed in the battle, the first military confrontation of the Revolution.

Americans. Learning of the British march, colonial riders—among them a silversmith named Paul Revere—galloped into the countryside to warn their countrymen.

By the time the British reached Lexington, a village on the road to Concord, a group of armed minutemen was waiting for them. Shots rang out, and seconds later, eight Americans lay dead on the village green. The British troops then moved on to Concord, where they destroyed the rebels' arsenal. Marching back to Boston, the redcoats ran into a hail of gunfire from American sharpshooters concealed behind fences, rocks, and trees. By the end of this eventful day (April 19) the

British had lost three times as many men as the Americans. The American Revolution had begun.

After Lexington and Concord, more than 10,000 Bostonians fled the city. Most of them were Tories—Americans who considered it treason to stage an armed insurrection against the British crown. One member of this group was John Wheatley, who reportedly moved to the nearby town of Chelsea. Another was his former slave, Phillis Wheatley.

The young woman's sympathies lay wholly with the Patriots; she probably left the city only at the urging of her former master. She went to stay in Providence, Rhode Island, with the Wheatleys' daughter, Mary, and her

Facing a troop of British soldiers, Concord's "embattled farmers" prepare to fire what poet Ralph Waldo Emerson later called "the shot heard round the world." The American Revolution had begun.

husband, John Lathrop, minister of a local church. It was while she was living in Providence that Phillis Wheatley wrote to George Washington.

The following year, 1776, would become the most famous in all American history, but it was a difficult one for Phillis Wheatley and her former owners. On March 17, 1776, a few days after her remarkable meeting with General George Washington, the British evac-

uated Boston. They left the city in turmoil.

Just before the British departure, the Wheatley mansion had been shattered by cannonading from across the harbor. Many other once proud and elegant Boston buildings also lay in rubble. British troops had chopped down trees and leveled many buildings, including the famous Old North Church, for firewood. The Old South

Meeting House, where Phillis Wheatley worshiped, was also badly damaged. "The pulpit, pews and seats [were] all cut to pieces and carried off in the most savage manner," reported an observer. "The beautiful carved pews with the silk furniture of Deacon Hubbards was taken down and carried [off] by an officer and made a hog sty."

In December 1776, Phillis Wheatley returned to Boston alone. The city where she had grown up was now a strange place. Most of her former supporters and acquaintances had fled. Even Captain Calef had gone back to London. Other friends and associates were dead. The few who remained were concentrating on keeping their lives together in a society torn by war and staggered by drastically rising prices.

By 1776, a loaf of bread cost three times as much as it had just three years earlier. The citizens who stayed in Boston found that the prices of food, clothing, and shelter were nearly beyond their means. The chaos and stress of the war had become compounded by an economic depression that affected virtually everyone.

Financially pressed or not, Phillis Wheatley's revolutionary fervor remained strong. On December 30, 1776, she wrote a poem praising Charles Lee, an American general who had recently been captured by the British. Compared with her ode to Washington of

Paul Revere was a skilled silversmith, but his fame rests on his April 18, 1775, "midnight ride" — a breakneck gallop through the countryside to warn his countrymen that the British were coming.

the previous year, this poem displays a sharpened sense of conflict and a more combative tone. In it, Lee speaks to his British captors:

Already, thousands of your troops are fled
To the drear mansions of the silent dead:
Columbia too, beholds with streaming eyes
Her heroes fall—'tis freedom's sacrifice!
So wills the power who with convulsive storms
Shakes impious realms, and nature's face deforms.

A whimsical contemporary cartoon depicts the June 1775 Battle of Bunker's Hill as "America's headdress." The British "won" the battle, but they lost 1,054 men to the Americans' 441.

Although there was no way she could have known it, Wheatley had made an unfortunate choice of heroes. Charles Lee, who bitterly resented being passed over for the assignment of commander in chief, had more than once disobeyed direct orders from Washington. It would later be revealed

Washington (center) raises his hand in ironic salute as the British evacuate Boston on March 17, 1776. When the Americans reentered the city, they found it in shambles.

Washington berates General Charles Lee (right) for disobeying orders in 1778. Wheatley miscalculated when she chose Lee, who was later accused of treason, as the subject of a heroic poem.

that while he was a British prisoner, Lee had betrayed the American cause by giving the British a secret plan to defeat the rebels.

Considering Lee's implacable hatred of Washington, the lines given him by the unsuspecting Wheatley were especially ironic. In the poem, Lee speaks "in praise of Godlike Washington," a "thrice happy chief in whom the virtues join."

Wheatley dedicated the Lee poem to Massachusetts patriot and future governor James Bowdoin. Aware of Lee's questionable loyalty and concerned about the poet's possible embarrassment, Bowdoin hid the poem. It was not published until 1863, when it was discovered among the statesman's papers.

As the war raged on, Wheatley's economic position grew more and more unsteady. John Wheatley died at the age of 72 early in 1778. He had been a wealthy man, but he did not mention Phillis Wheatley in his will. Soon after his demise, his daughter Mary also died. Phillis Wheatley left no record of her feelings about these losses, but they must have troubled her deeply.

She had grown up with the Wheatleys and had always depended on them for guidance. Now three of them were gone. Only Nathaniel remained; and he was married and managing the family business in London, thousands of miles away. (Nathaniel would die in 1783; like his father, he would fail to name the Wheatley family's former slave in his will.)

Phillis Wheatley was facing hard times. She was no longer an exotic African child prodigy. She was a free black woman in her mid-twenties with no marketable skills. There were no more prominent white patrons to sponsor her, no more wealthy intellectuals to invite her to tea and celebrate her talent for reflecting their safe, civilized, and God-fearing world. Of the 18 men who had signed the statement vouching for her authorship, nearly half were dead. The rest were too deeply involved in the war to worry about poets or poetry.

For the first time since her arrival in America, nearly 17 years earlier, Phillis Wheatley was alone, with nothing and no one to catch her if she stumbled. It

Statesman and patriot James Bowdoin, a longtime admirer of Wheatley, realized that her poem about Charles Lee could hurt her reputation. He prevented its publication.

would have been difficult to find a worse time to be in her predicament. In the chaotic wartime economy, even skilled black workers were finding it hard to earn money. The chances of success for a black woman whose only asset was her art would be faint indeed. Clearly, something had to be done.

As Washington prepares to review his troops, a young black soldier holds the reins of his horse. Ignoring tradition, Washington authorized the enlistment of blacks in 1775.

SEVEN

Marriage and Independence

In the spring of 1778, Phillis Wheatley was alone in a troubled, war-torn world. Facing a society indifferent to her art and threatening to her very survival, she took a major step: she got married. Although this was perhaps the most independent move of her life, many of those who knew her thought it was a serious mistake.

Her new husband was John Peters, the man who had sometimes acted as her messenger to Obour Tanner. In a letter to Tanner, Wheatley had called Peters "complaisant and agreeable." Not everyone agreed with that description; some people said he was "shiftless" and "demanding." Others, however, characterized him as "ambitious" and "brilliant."

Wheatley and Peters posted a legal notice of their intent to marry on April 1, a few days after the death of the elderly John Wheatley. The announcement listed both the poet and her husband-to-be as "free Negroes." History retains only a shadowy impression of Peters, and the picture of Wheatley's life with him is similarly cloudy. Much less is known about her married life than about her earlier days, when her literary gifts were celebrated by white society in both England and America. After her marriage to Peters, she maintained little contact with her former acquaintances. No white biographers or family friends were near to record her experiences, and she herself had never been inclined to make public statements about her private life.

Nevertheless, some facts are clear. Obour Tanner, for example, left no doubt about her sentiments toward John Peters. Many years later, a white woman who knew Tanner reported on a conversation with her at her home in

The Bucks of America, an all-black Massachusetts company, carried this flag into battle during the Revolution. Of the 300,000 men who fought for American independence, about 5,000 were black.

Newport, Rhode Island. "Obour informed me, pious soul that she was," said this informant in a letter to a friend, "that 'Poor Phillis let herself down by marrying.'"

The letter writer went on to speculate that Tanner's disapproval might have been the result of "her own condition of single blessedness"—in other words, jealousy. She said, however, that she doubted this theory, "as I heard the same thing expressed frequently by old people in Newport who remembered the circumstances."

The conversation between Tanner and the letter writer took place about 1830, a few years before Tanner's death. She was, said the writer, "an uncommonly pious, sensible, and intelligent woman, respected and visited by every person in Newport who could appreciate excellence."

John Peters was thoroughly disliked by at least some members of the

A visiting German officer sketched these American military uniforms in 1782. Supplies, however, were scarce; many officers and most enlisted men wore their own clothes on duty.

Wheatley family. Biographer Margaretta Odell reported that Wheatley relatives who knew the poet conceded that Peters was "a man of talents and information," but insisted that he was "disagreeable." The relatives told Odell that, "on account of his improper conduct, Phillis became entirely estranged from the immediate family."

In his 1916 book, *The Life and Works of Phillis Wheatley*, G. Herbert Renfro quotes another view of Peters. He was, said a contemporary observer, "a respectable colored man of Boston," who "kept a grocery in Court Street and was a man of handsome person. He wore a wig, carried a cane, and quite 'acted out the gentleman.'"

A white schoolmaster bars the admission of black students in this illustration from an early 19th-century abolitionist journal. Such publications multiplied after the Revolution.

Jane Tyler Lathrop, daughter of Mary Wheatley and granddaughter of Susannah, described Peters as "not only a very remarkable looking man, but a man of letters and information [who] wrote with fluency and propriety, and at one time read law."

The archives of the Massachusetts Historical Society contain a report that Peters "practiced law, or professed to." Unlike the South, which allowed blacks no legal rights, the North gave blacks, both free and slave, almost the same legal protection as whites. A slave could testify against his master and could even give evidence in cases between two whites.

Peters apparently acted as a legal advocate who, according to one witness, "pleaded the cause of his brethren, the Africans, before the tribunals [courts] of the state." This observer noted that "Peters not only bore a good character, but was in every way a remarkable specimen of his race, being a fluent writer, a ready speaker and an intelligent man."

One report in the Massachusetts Historical Society says that Peters "felt himself superior to labor." Another labels him as "shiftless." These, however, were the views of a white attorney, who might have considered it presumptuous for a black man to present himself on an equal footing in a law court.

Peters achieved some success in a variety of occupations; he was reported to have worked not only as a lawyer and a grocer, but as a barber, a baker, and even a doctor. The practice of so many occupations hardly suggests a "shiftless" man. Perhaps "daring" and "ambitious" might have been better words for him.

Although other people expressed their opinions of her husband and her marriage, Wheatley herself left no direct testimony on the subjects. On May 29, 1778, only a few weeks after her wedding, she wrote Tanner after a long period of silence. The letter is hardly more than a hasty note, its contents philosophical rather than personal: "The vast variety of scenes that have passed before us these 3 years past, will to a reasonable mind serve to convince us of the uncertain duration of all things temporal. . . . "

Signed "Phillis Wheatley" (not Peters), the letter mentions neither its author's newfound freedom nor her marriage. It may, in fact, be more revealing for what it leaves out than for what it says. For a freedwoman with a new husband, it shows a remarkable absence of joy or excitement. But it should be remembered that Wheatley had not been trained for either freedom or marriage. Neither would bring her happiness. Perhaps she already sensed this.

Nearly a year later, on May 10, 1779, she wrote to Tanner again. This time she used her married name, signing herself "your friend and sister, Phillis Peters." She was now expecting a baby, but she made no reference to it. Instead, the letter conveyed a sense of hardship and resignation, as though her life had become a struggle. "Tho' I have been silent," she wrote, "I have not been unmindful of you, but a variety of hindrances was the cause of my not writing to you."

At the end of this letter Wheatley said, "In time to come I hope our correspondence will revive—and revive in better times— pray write me soon, for I long to hear from you—you may depend on constant replies. I wish you much happiness." The "constant replies," however, were not to appear. This letter was apparently the last Tanner ever received from her friend.

As she awaited the birth of her first child, Wheatley wrote a prayer entitled "Sabbath, June 13, 1779." In it, she asked God to give her "strength to bring forth living and perfect a being who shall be greatly instrumental in promoting thy [glory]." Sadly, her hopes were not to be realized; the child died soon after birth.

Four months later, Wheatley tried to arrange for the publication of a second volume of poems. From October to December 1779 she paid for a series of notices in Boston's *Evening Post and General Advertiser*, soliciting subscribers for the proposed book. It would, said the notices, be "dedicated to the Right Honourable Benjamin Franklin, Esq." She ran the proposal under her married name and described herself as a "female African." The advertisements promised a collection of 33 poems and

"The horse America, throwing his master," a contemporary British cartoon, mocks King George's loss of the American colonies. Many Britons sympathized with the colonists' fight for independence.

13 letters. Of the poems listed, only the ode to Washington had been published before.

Wheatley continued to have a certain literary reputation, but this was 1779, not 1773. The war raged on, and Boston was still suffering its effects. Few people had money to spare for such luxuries as expensive books of poetry. "It must be remembered," wrote Margaretta Odell, "that this was a season of general poverty. Phillis's friends of former days were scattered far and wide. Many of them, attached to the royal interest [sympathetic to the British], had left the country."

Wheatley's second book was never published, although five of the poems and a few of the letters later appeared in print. Most of the others have disappeared.

Despite this rejection, Wheatley and her husband were living quite comfortably. Boston records show that after 1780, when Massachusetts abolished slavery, the Peters family lived in a house on fashionable Queen Street (now Court Street). This was an enviable neighborhood for any citizen, white or black.

Peters's real-estate taxes on the Queen Street house were an impressive £150, which indicates that it was no ordinary, modest dwelling. Peters was one of a handful of free blacks who owned property in Boston, but judging from real-estate records of the time, his

Most 18th-century reading material — including some of Phillis Wheatley's poems — was printed on presses like this one, an example of Benjamin Franklin's many innovative designs.

was by far the most expensive house. Even Prince Hall, a well-known black minister and revolutionary soldier who would later found the Negro Masonic Order, paid only about £16 in taxes on his home.

Wheatley may have had a fashion-

Revolutionary War veteran Prince Hall, a neighbor of the Peters family, was an abolitionist, the founder of the black Masonic order, and a crusader for improved education for black children.

able address, but there is no evidence that it brought her joy. Her last letters to Tanner suggest that she was enduring illnesses and other difficulties, which allowed her little time to write either letters or poems. Her spirits must also have been dampened by her failure to interest subscribers for her book.

Nevertheless, she was not quite forgotten. On August 4, 1778, Jupiter Hammon, a slave who lived with his master in Hartford, Connecticut, published a 21-verse poem. It was addressed to "Miss Phillis Wheatley, Ethiopean Poetess, in Boston, who came from Africa at eight years of age, and soon became acquainted with the Gospel of Jesus Christ." If Wheatley read Hammon's poem, perhaps it lifted her spirits. It included these verses:

> Come, dear Phillis, be advised,
> To drink Samaria's flood;
> There's nothing that shall suffice
> But Christ's redeeming blood.
> While thousands muse with earthly toys;
> And range beyond the street,
> Dear Phillis, seek for heaven's joys,
> Where we do hope to meet.

The British army surrenders after the decisive American victory at Yorktown, Virginia, on October 19, 1781. A few minor battles remained to be fought, but the Revolution was effectively over.

EIGHT

Struggle and Tragedy

The Peters family moved out of Boston in the early 1780s. The family, now consisting of John, his wife, Phillis, and a child born after the death of their first infant in 1779, settled in the village of Wilmington, north of the city. Although no records remain of John Peters's business dealings, he had probably been forced to move because of financial troubles.

The resulting change in life-style must have been drastic. Gone was the excitement of life in Boston, a sophisticated and lively city even in wartime. Gone was the elegant house on Queen Street, along with the ease it provided. Wilmington was a small and relatively primitive country town, offering few comforts or diversions.

That the poet had once been a "Wheatley" counted for little in Wilmington. Now she was just Mrs. John Peters, a poor black freedwoman little

different on the surface from many others. Now there were no rests in the country or ocean voyages to help her recover from her frequent bouts of illness.

Although she had grown up as a slave, Wheatley had not been trained to endure a life of physical hardship. Her former masters had assigned her few chores and many special privileges. As she had observed in a letter to Obour Tanner, Susannah Wheatley had treated her more like her own child than like a servant. The harshness of life in the village took its toll, leaving Wheatley in increasingly fragile health.

In 1781, British general Charles Cornwallis surrendered to General George Washington in Yorktown, Virginia. Although the treaty officially ending the long conflict was not signed until 1783, the American Revolution

Bostonians cheer the news of Cornwallis's surrender. One long ordeal was over, but more hard work lay ahead — the restoration of the new nation's war-torn economy.

was over. Nevertheless, life in the colonies, particularly for the poor, continued to be hard.

John Peters apparently found it impossible to support his family in Wilmington, and soon after the end of the war they decided to return to Boston.

Wheatley and her child went first, moving in with Elizabeth Wallcut, a niece of Susannah Wheatley. Wallcut operated a day school for "young Misses," where the poet may have given lessons to help pay for her room and board.

At the end of six weeks, Peters arrived in Boston to install his family in what a contemporary observer called "an obscure part of town." It was probably a dismal neighborhood; by the late 18th century, segregated black ghettos had already begun to sprout up in many New England communities. Like their mother, Wheatley's children were frail. Soon after her resettlement in Boston, her second child died. She was, however, soon pregnant again.

Somehow, John Peters seems to have raised enough money to try his hand at yet another occupation. On July 28, 1784, he applied for a license permitting the sale of liquor at a shop—apparently his own—on Prince Street. Since such stores rented for nearly £30 a year, his fortunes had obviously taken a turn for the better.

In his license petition, Peters explained that he had opened the shop "for the purpose of supporting self and family." The petition included testimony signed by the Boston town clerk, William Cooper. He was the brother of Samuel Cooper, the minister who had baptized Phillis Wheatley at the Old South Meeting House in 1771. William Cooper's statement said, "The Selectmen of Boston hereby certify that the within named petitioner [is] a person of sober life and conversation suitably qualified and provided for the exercise of the employment of a retailer of spiritous liquors."

While this document indicates that

Wheatley had long admired Samuel Cooper, the Congregational minister who had baptized her in 1771. The elegy she wrote on his death in 1784 was her first published work in almost a decade.

Peters was far from destitute, other evidence shows that he continued to have serious financial problems. According to Massachusetts Historical Society records, in 1784 "he was forced to relieve himself of debt by an imprisonment in the county jail."

Peters later paid off some of his debts by selling Wheatley's books. Among

"Reconciliation between Britannia and her daughter America" was a popular postwar cartoon. *"Dear Mama, say no more about it,"* says America. The reply: *"Be a good girl and give me a buss [kiss]."*

them was the symbol of her most triumphant hour—the copy of *Paradise Lost* she had received from the lord mayor of London in 1773. (This volume is now in the Harvard University library.)

Whatever her husband's successes and failures, Wheatley once again emerged as a published author in 1784. In January she published a six-page pamphlet containing an elegy to Samuel Cooper, who had recently died. Cooper, one of the 18 distinguished Bostonians who had signed the statement verifying her authorship of *Poems on Various Subjects*, had remained her personal and literary supporter throughout his life.

"Occasional" poems (those written to commemorate events) were very popular in the 18th century. Such poems were often elegies, a form in which Wheatley had demonstrated her talent many times. In September the *Boston Magazine* contained another elegy, this one addressed to parents whose infant son had recently died.

By the time this poem was published, its author had lost two of her own children, but her lines reflect no sense of personal loss. Again, this was typical of the time; poets were not expected to demonstrate any strong feelings of individual joy and sorrow. Their job was to create dignified and formal expressions of universal experience.

By the late fall of 1784, Phillis Wheatley had given birth to her third child. She had also just finished writing her last poem, "Liberty and Peace," which celebrated the end of the war that had so radically altered her life. Beginning with the line, "Lo! Freedom comes," the poem is an outpouring of unabashed patriotism, an emotional tribute to America's emergence as a free nation. To prove she had always been sure of the American victory, she included a few lines from her ode to George Washington, written in 1776.

The optimistic tone of "Liberty and Peace" is typified by its closing lines:

So Freedom comes arrayed with charms divine,
And in her train commerce and plenty shine.

The poem was published in late December 1784, but Phillis Wheatley never saw it in print. By the time it appeared, she was dead.

Phillis Wheatley's last months had been spent in poverty and loneliness. Her husband was away, probably in debtor's prison, and "she, poor Phillis," according to a Historical Society document, "was obliged to earn her own subsistence in a common Negro boarding house."

In Boston and London, Phillis Wheatley had been celebrated for her literary gifts. George Washington, now the hero of his nation, had applauded her work and expressed his desire "to

The body of the young Lady, loft in Capt. Copeland's floop, on Cohaffet rocks, as lately mentioned in this paper, has fince been found, and decently interred.

MARRIED, at her Father's Manfion, in Duxbury, by the Rev. Mr. Sanger, the amiable Mifs NABBY ALDEN, youngeft Daughter of Colonel Briggs Alden, of that Place, to Mr. BEZA HAYWARD, of Bridgewater.

Laft Lord's day died, Mrs. PHILLIS PETERS, (formerly Phillis Wheatly) aged 31, known to the literary world by her celebrated mifcellaneous Poems. Her funeral is to be this afternoon, at 4 o'clock, from the houfe lately improved by Mr. Todd, nearly oppofite Dr. Bulfinch's, at Weft-Bofton, where her friends and acquaintance are defired to attend.

NAVAL-OFFICE, Bofton, December 9.
ENTERED.

Brig	Harriot,	Sturgifs,	New-York.
——	Independence,	Bondi,	Martinico.
Sloop	S____ & Polly,	Sturgifs,	New-York.
——	R____,	Godfrey,	N. Carolina.
——	Maria,	Parker,	Richmond.

CLEARED.

Brig	Betfey,	Clement,	Cape-Francois
Sloop	Pilgrim,	LaMoyne,	Lifbon,
Scho.	Kingfton,	Tittle,	Mole.

Among the public notices in the December 8, 1784, issue of the Massachusetts Independent Chronicle and Universal Advertiser *was an announcement of the recent death of Phillis Peters.*

Abraham Lincoln reads the Emancipation Proclamation to his cabinet. The liberation of America's slaves took place in 1863, a century after Phillis Wheatley had arrived on a slave ship.

see a person so favored by the Muses, and to whom nature has been so liberal and beneficent in her dispensations." But all this had happened long ago.

Now, exhausted by heavy work, illness, and childbirth, the poet spent her days in a grim residence for the poor. Her long ordeal came to an end on December 5, 1784. At the age of 31, she died in her boarding-house bed. Her sole companion was her third child, who joined her in death only a few hours afterward.

Three days later, a small notice appeared in the *Massachusetts Independent Chronicle and Universal Advertiser*: "Last Lord's Day, died Mrs. Phillis Peters (formerly Phillis Wheatley), aged 31, known to the world by her celebrated miscellaneous poems. Her funeral is to be this afternoon, at four o'clock.... Her friends and acquaintances are desired to attend."

Despite the announcement, no mourners came to the poet's funeral service. She was, according to one witness, "carried to her last earthly resting-place, without one of her friends of her prosperity to follow her, and without a stone to mark her grave." Her child was buried beside her.

We will never know what thoughts, what unrealized dreams haunted the final days of Phillis Wheatley. Perhaps she was still able to find comfort in the imagination from which she had created her poetry, and which she celebrated in lines that might serve as her epitaph:

> Imagination! who can sing thy force?
> Or who describe the swiftness of thy
> course?
> Soaring through air to find the bright
> abode,
> The empyreal palace of the thundering
> God,
> We on thy pinions can surpass the
> wind,
> And leave the rolling universe behind.

Wheatley came from an unknown village in West Africa. She was buried in an unmarked grave in America. She spent her life struggling first for recognition and then for mere survival, and she died alone. Nevertheless, she left her mark on American history.

She had overcome enormous obstacles in order to leave that mark. She was a woman in a society that confined women to the hearth and the parlor. She was a black in a country that enslaved and oppressed black people. She wrote in a language not originally her own, and in it, composed poetry that ranked with the best work of many of her American contemporaries.

Wheatley and her poetry were virtually ignored for several decades after her death. Interest in her was revived in the mid-19th century, when she became a symbol of the abolition movement. Attempting to put an end to slavery, abolitionists maintained that the accomplishments of such artists as Wheatley disproved the ancient lie that blacks were an inferior race and, therefore, fit only to be slaves.

After Abraham Lincoln's Emancipation Proclamation finally freed America's slaves in 1863, Wheatley's works once again fell into a period of obscurity. As black Americans of this century assert and redefine their identity, however, Phillis Wheatley has once again become an important figure in American letters.

Her burial place in Boston remains unknown, but the city now contains an impressive monument to her. On February 1, 1985, a little more than 200 years after her death, the arts and sciences building at the University of Massachusetts was dedicated as Wheatley Hall. Massachusetts governor Michael Dukakis proclaimed February 1 as Phillis Wheatley Day, honoring the woman who is recognized as the mother of black literature in this country—the first black, the first slave, and the second woman to publish a book in what was to become the United States of America.

Celebrating "Phillis Wheatley Day" in 1985, Massachusetts officials unveil a portrait of the author. It was based on a 1773 etching, the only known likeness of America's first black poet.

FURTHER READING

Brawley, Benjamin. *Early Negro American Writers*. Chapel Hill, NC: The University of North Carolina Press, 1935.

———. *Negro Builders and Heroes*. Chapel Hill, NC: The University of North Carolina Press, 1937.

Franklin, John Hope. *From Slavery to Freedom: A History of Negro Americans*. New York: Knopf, 1980.

Greene, Lorenzo Johnston. *The Negro in Colonial New England, 1620–1776*. New York: Columbia University Press, 1942.

Kaplan, Sidney. *The Black Presence in the Era of the American Revolution, 1770–1800*. Greenwich, CT: New York Graphic Society, 1973.

Loggins, Vernon. *The Negro Author: His Development in America to 1900*. New York: Columbia University Press, 1931.

Mannix, Daniel P. *Black Cargoes*. New York: Viking, 1962.

Mason, Julian D., Jr. *The Poems of Phillis Wheatley*. Chapel Hill: The University of North Carolina Press, 1966.

Odell, Margaretta Matilda. *Memoir and Poems of Phillis Wheatley*. Boston: George W. Light, 1834.

Pennsylvania Magazine. April, 1776.

Renfro, G. Herbert. *Life and Works of Phillis Wheatley*. Freeport, NY: Books for Libraries Press, 1970.

Richmond, Merle. *Bid the Vassal Soar: Interpretive Essays on the Life and Poetry of Phillis Wheatley and George Moses Horton*. Washington, D.C.: Howard University Press, 1974.

Robinson, William H. *Critical Essays on Phillis Wheatley*. Boston: G. K. Hall, 1982.

———. *Phillis Wheatley and Her Writings*. New York: Garland Publishing, 1984.

Van Doren, Carl. *Secret History of the American Revolution*. New York: Viking, 1941.

CHRONOLOGY

c. 1754	Phillis Wheatley born, probably in Senegambia, West Africa
1761	Kidnapped by slavers
	Arrives in Boston aboard slaveship *Phillis* and is purchased by Susannah Wheatley, wife of a wealthy merchant
1761–70	Learns English, studies literature and Latin, and begins to compose poetry
	Is invited into the homes of upper-class Bostonians to recite her poetry
1768	British troops arrive in Boston to quell colonial unrest
	Wheatley writes a poem: "On the Arrival of the Ships of War, and Landing of the Troops"
1771	Composes first major work, an elegy to evangelist George Whitefield
1772	Susannah Wheatley arranges London publication of Wheatley's poems
	Prominent Bostonians verify the book's author as a black
1773	Wheatley visits England, where she is enthusiastically received
	Returns to Boston when Susannah Wheatley becomes ill
	Poems on Various Subjects, Religious and Moral is published in London amid great fanfare and sells well. Britons praise the book but criticize Americans for keeping its author enslaved
1774	Wheatley writes letter repudiating slavery, which is reprinted throughout New England
	Susannah Wheatley dies
1775	Wheatley writes "Reply," the first recorded celebration of an African heritage by a black American
	Moves to Providence, Rhode Island, as American Revolution begins
	Sends General George Washington a poem in his honor
1776	Meets with Washington at his Cambridge, Massachusetts, headquarters
	Returns to Boston after British troops evacuate the city
1778	Marries John Peters, a struggling black businessman
1779	Bears the first of three children, all of whom die in infancy
	Launches an unsuccessful drive to gain subscribers for a second book of poetry
1783	American Revolution ends
1784	Wheatley writes final poem, "Liberty and Peace," celebrating the end of the war
Dec. 5, 1784	Phillis Wheatley dies destitute in a Boston boardinghouse

INDEX

PICTURE CREDITS

The Bettmann Archive: pp. 14, 17, 32, 36, 38, 43, 54, 62, 68, 81, 82,
84, 96, 98, 100, 103; The Boston Society Old State House: pp. 29,
30, 48, 51, 72, 90, 93; Essex Institute: p. 35; The Houghton Library, Harvard University: p. 42; Library of Congress: pp. 4, 12, 15,
18, 19, 20, 28, 37, 44, 46, 52, 59, 63, 64, 66, 76, 79, 80, 83, 85, 86, 89,
92, 102; Massachusetts Historical Society: pp. 16, 24, 25, 40, 47, 53,
56, 58, 70, 71, 74, 88, 99; National Portrait Gallery: p. 60; New
London County Historical Society: p. 69; The Peabody Museum
of Salem: pp. 23, 26, 27, 75; Schomburg Center for Research in
Black Culture: p. 94; UMASS/Boston Photo: p. 105

Merle Richmond is the author of *Bid the Vassal Soar: Interpretive Essays on the Life and Poetry of Phillis Wheatley and George Moses Horton*. She received her bachelor's and master's degrees from the University of California at Berkeley. She lives with her husband and two sons in San Francisco.

Matina S. Horner is president of Radcliffe College and associate professor of psychology and social relations at Harvard University. She is best known for her studies of women's motivation, achievement, and personality development. Dr. Horner serves on several national boards and advisory councils, including those of the National Science Foundation, Time Inc., and the Women's Research and Education Institute. She earned her B. A. from Bryn Mawr College and Ph.D. from the University of Michigan, and holds honorary degrees from many colleges and universities, including Mount Holyoke, Smith, Tufts, and the University of Pennsylvania.